D1359928

Marianne Moore

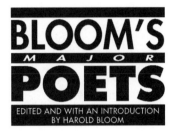

CURRENTLY AVAILABLE

Marianne Moore

CHELSEA HOUSE
P U B L I S H E R S
A Haights Cross Communications Company
Philadelphia

EDITED AND WITH AN INTRODUCTION
BY HAROLD BLOOM

First Printing
1 3 5 7 9 8 6 4 2

Library of Congress Cataloging-in-Publication Data

Marianne Moore / edited and with an introduction by Harold Bloom.
    p. cm. -- (Bloom's major poets)
  Includes bibliographical references and index.
  ISBN 0-7910-7890-6
  1. Moore, Marianne, 1887-1972--Criticism and interpretation. 2.
Women and literature--United States--History--20th century. I. Bloom,
Harold. II. Series.
  PS3525.O5616Z689 2003
  811'.52--dc22

                                           2003024089

Chelsea House Publishers
1974 Sproul Road, Suite 400
Broomall, PA 19008-0914

www.chelseahouse.com

Contributing Editor: Camille-Yvette Welsch
Cover design by Keith Trego
Layout by EJB Publishing Services

CONTENTS

USER'S GUIDE

This volume is designed to present biographical, critical, and bibliographical information on the author and the author's best-known or most important poems. Following Harold Bloom's editor's note and introduction is a concise biography of the author that discusses major life events and important literary accomplishments. A critical analysis of each poem follows, tracing significant themes, patterns, and motifs in the work. As with any study guide, it is recommended that the reader read the poem beforehand and have a copy of the poem being discussed available for quick reference.

A selection of critical extracts, derived from previously published material, follows each thematic analysis. In most cases, these extracts represent the best analysis available from a number of leading critics. Because these extracts are derived from previously published material, they will include the original notations and references when available. Each extract is cited, and readers are encouraged to check the original publication as they continue their research. A bibliography of the author's writings, a list of additional books and articles on the author and their work, and an index of themes and ideas conclude the volume.

ABOUT THE EDITOR

Harold Bloom is Sterling Professor of the Humanities at Yale University and Henry W. and Albert A. Berg Professor of English at the New York University Graduate School. He is the author of over 20 books, and the editor of more than 30 anthologies of literary criticism.

Professor Bloom's works include *Shelley's Mythmaking* (1959), *The Visionary Company* (1961), *Blake's Apocalypse* (1963), *Yeats* (1970), *A Map of Misreading* (1975), *Kabbalah and Criticism* (1975), *Agon: Toward a Theory of Revisionism* (1982), *The American Religion* (1992), *The Western Canon* (1994), and *Omens of Millennium: The Gnosis of Angels, Dreams, and Resurrection* (1996). *The Anxiety of Influence* (1973) sets forth Professor Bloom's provocative theory of the literary relationships between the great writers and their predecessors. His most recent books include *Shakespeare: The Invention of the Human*, a 1998 National Book Award finalist, *How to Read and Why* (2000), *Stories and Poems for Extremely Intelligent Children of All Ages* (2001), *Genius: A Mosaic of One Hundred Exemplary Creative Minds* (2002), and *Hamlet: Poem Unlimited* (2003).

Professor Bloom earned his Ph.D. from Yale University in 1955 and has served on the Yale faculty since then. He is a 1985 MacArthur Foundation Award recipient and served as the Charles Eliot Norton Professor of Poetry at Harvard University in 1987–88. In 1999 he was awarded the prestigious American Academy of Arts and Letters Gold Medal for Criticism. Professor Bloom is the editor of several other Chelsea House series in literary criticism, including BLOOM'S MAJOR SHORT STORY WRITERS, BLOOM'S MAJOR NOVELISTS, BLOOM'S MAJOR DRAMATISTS, BLOOM'S MODERN CRITICAL INTERPRETATIONS, BLOOM'S MODERN CRITICAL VIEWS, BLOOM'S BIOCRITIQUES, BLOOM'S GUIDES, BLOOM'S MAJOR LITERARY CHARACTERS, and BLOOM'S PERIOD STUDIES.

EDITOR'S NOTE

My Introduction interprets Marianne Moore's masterwork, the collage-poem "Marriage."

As there are thirty-three Critical Views here of four major poems of Marianne Moore, I will confine these remarks to a few that seem to me of high usefulness.

Bonnie Costello brings "The Steeple-Jack" together with Albrecht Dürer, while John Slatin shows Hawthorne's effect on the poem.

"The Fish" is illuminated by the Formalism of Hugh Kenner, and the attention to poetic syntax by Cristanne Miller.

Perhaps Moore's most famous work, "Poetry" is analyzed by the superb New Critic R.P. Blackmur, and by E.R. Gregory.

Among the thirteen perspectives upon "Marriage," I particularly commend those by Pamela White Hadas, and Heather Cass White.

Harold Bloom

I

For Plato the only reality that mattered is exemplified best for us in the principles of mathematics. The aim of our lives should be to draw ourselves away as much as possible from the unsubstantial, fluctuating facts of the world about us and establish some communion with the objects which are apprehended by thought and not sense. This was the source of Plato's asceticism. To the extent that Miss Moore finds only allusion tolerable she shares that asceticism. While she shares it she does so only as it may be necessary for her to do so in order to establish a particular reality or, better, a reality of her own particulars.
                                                      —WALLACE STEVENS

Allusion was Marianne Moore's method, a method that was her self. One of the most American of all poets, she was fecund in her progeny—Elizabeth Bishop, May Swenson, and Richard Wilbur being the most gifted among them. Her own American precursors were not Emily Dickinson and Walt Whitman—still our two greatest poets—but the much slighter Stephen Crane, who is echoed in her earliest poems, and in an oblique way Edgar Poe, whom she parodied. I suspect that her nearest poetic father, in English, was Thomas Hardy, who seems to have taught her lessons in the mastery of incongruity, and whose secularized version of Biblical irony is not far from her own. If we compare her with her major poetic contemporaries—Frost, Stevens, Eliot, Pound, Williams, Aiken, Ransom, Cummings, H.D., Hart Crane—she is clearly the most original American poet of her era, though not quite of the eminence of Frost, Stevens, Crane. A curious kind of devotional poet, with some authentic affinities to George Herbert, she reminds us implicitly but constantly that any distinction between sacred and secular poetry is only a shibboleth of cultural politics. Some day she will remind us also of what current cultural politics obscure: that any distinction between poetry written by women or poetry by men is a mere polemic, unless it follows upon an initial distinction between good and bad poetry. Moore, like Bishop and Swenson, is an extraordinary poet-as-poet. The issue of how gender enters into her vision should arise only after the aesthetic achievement is judged as such.

Moore, as all her readers know, to their lasting delight, is the visionary of natural creatures: the jerboa, frigate pelican, buffalo, monkeys, fish, snakes, mongooses, the octopus (actually a trope for a mountain), snail, peacock, whale, pangolin, wood-weasel, elephants, race horses, chameleon, jellyfish, arctic ox (or goat), giraffe, blue bug (another trope, this time for a pony), all of La Fontaine's bestiary, not to mention sea and land unicorns, basilisks, and all the weird fabulous roster that perhaps only Borges also, among crucial modern writers, celebrates so consistently. There is something of Blake and of the Christopher Smart of *Jubilate Agno* in Moore, though the affinity does not result from influence, but rather is the consequence of election. Moore's famous eye, like that of Bishop after her, is not so much a visual gift as it is visionary, for the beasts in her poems are charged with a spiritual intensity that doubtless they possess, but which I myself cannot see without the aid of Blake, Smart, and Moore.

I remember always in reading Moore again that her favorite poem was the Book of Job. Just as I cannot read Ecclesiastes without thinking of Dr. Johnson, I cannot read certain passages in Job without recalling Marianne Moore:

> But ask now the beasts, and they shall teach thee; and the fowls of the air, and they shall tell thee:
> Or speak to the earth, and it shall teach thee: and the fishes of the sea shall declare unto thee.
> Who knoweth not in all these that the hand of the Lord hath wrought this?
> In whose hand is the soul of every living thing.

This, from chapter 12, is the prelude to the great chant of Yahweh, the Voice out of the whirlwind that sounds forth in the frightening magnificence of chapters 38 through 41, where the grand procession of beasts comprehends lions, ravens, wild goats, the wild ass, the unicorn, peacocks, the ostrich, the sublime battle-horse who "saith among the trumpets, Ha, ha," the hawk, the eagle, and at last behemoth and leviathan. Gorgeously celebrating his own creation, Yahweh through the poet of job engendered another strong poet in Marianne Moore. Of the Book of job, she remarked that its agony was veracious and its fidelity of a force "that contrives glory for ashes."

"Glory for ashes" might be called Moore's ethical motto, the basis for the drive of her poetic will toward a reality of her own particulars. Her poetry, as befitted the translator of La Fontaine, and the heir of George Herbert, would be in some danger of dwindling into moral essays, an impossible form for our time, were it not for her wild allusiveness, her zest for quotations, and her essentially anarchic stance, the American and Emersonian insistence upon seeing everything in her own way, with "conscientious inconsistency." When her wildness or freedom subsided, she produced an occasional poetic disaster like the patriotic war poems "In Distrust of Merits" and "'Keeping Their World Large.'" But her greatest poems are at just the opposite edge of consciousness: "A Grave," "Novices," "Marriage," "An Octopus," "He 'Digesteth Harde Yron,'" "Elephants," the deceptively light "Tom Fool at Jamaica."

Those seven poems by themselves have an idiosyncratic splendor that restores my faith, as a critic, in what the language of the poets truly is: diction, or choice of words, playing endlessly upon the dialectic of denotation and connotation, a dialectic that simply vanishes in all Structuralist and post-Structuralist ruminations upon the supposed priority of "language" over meaning. "The arbitrariness of the signifier" loses its charm when one asks a Gallic psycholinguistifier whether denotation or connotation belongs to the signifier, as opposed to the signified, and one beholds blank incredulity as one's only answer. Moore's best poems give the adequate reply: the play of the signifier is answered always by the play of the signified, because the play of diction, or the poet's will over language, is itself constituted by the endless interchanges of denotation and connotation. Moore, with her rage to order allusion, echo, and quotation in ghostlier demarcations, keener sounds, helps us to realize that the belated Modernism of the Gallic proclamation of the death of the author was no less premature than it was, always already, belated.

Marriage, through which thought does not penetrate, appeared to Miss Moore a legitimate object for art, an art that would not halt from using thought about it, however, as it might want to. Against marriage, "this institution, perhaps one should say enterprise"—Miss Moore launched her thought not to have it appear arsenaled as in a textbook on psychology, but to stay among apples and giraffes in a poem.
—WILLIAM CARLOS WILLIAMS

If I had to cite a single poem by Moore as representing all of her powers working together, it would be "Marriage" (1923), superficially an outrageous collage but profoundly a poignant comic critique of every society's most sacred and tragic institution. As several critics have ventured, this is Moore's *The Waste Land*, a mosaic of fragments from Francis Bacon, the *Scientific American*, Baxter's *The Saint's Everlasting Rest*, Hazlitt on Burke, William Godwin, Trollope, *The Tempest*, a book on *The Syrian Christ*, the Bible, Ezra Pound, and even Daniel Webster (from an inscription on a statue!), and twenty sources more. Yet it is a poem, and perhaps is more ruggedly unified than any other poem of such ambition by Moore.

The poet's own headnote to "Marriage" could not be more diffident: "Statements that took my fancy which I tried to arrange plausibly." The arrangement is more than plausible; it is quite persuasive, though it begins with a parody of the societal *apologia* for marriage:

This institution,
perhaps one should say enterprise
out of respect for which
one says one need not change one's mind
about a thing one has believed in,
requiring public promises
of one's intention
to fulfill a private obligation.

No one, I believe, could interpret that opening stance with

any exactitude. The substitution of "enterprise" for "institution" qualifies the wryness of "public promises / of one's intention / to fulfill a private obligation," but adds a note both of commerce and of the human virtue of taking an initiative. Who could have anticipated that the next movement of the poem would be this?

I wonder what Adam and Eve
think of it by this time,
this fire-gilt steel
alive with goldenness;
how bright it shows—
"of circular traditions and impostures,
committing many spoils,"
requiring all one's criminal ingenuity
to avoid!

Like nearly every other quotation in this poem, the two lines from Sir Francis Bacon gain nothing for Moore's own text by being restored to their own context. Steel burned by fire does not exactly brighten into a golden bough, so the "gilt" is there partly as anticipation of "criminal ingenuity." Yet "gilt" is in cognitive sequence with "goldenness" and "bright," even if we rightly expect to behold blackened steel. All who have known marriage (as Moore declined to do) will register an unhappy shudder at the force the Baconian phrases take on when Moore appropriates them. Traditions as treasons become circular, and together with impostures can be read here either as performing many despoilments or as investing many gains of previous despoilments. Either way, it might seem as though an ingenuity avoiding this equivocal enterprise could only be taken as criminal by some dogmatist, whether societal or theological.

The poem proceeds to dismiss psychology, since to explain everything is to explain nothing, and then meditates upon the beauty, talents, and contrariness of Eve, a meditation that suddenly achieves Paterian intensity:

Below the incandescent stars
below the incandescent fruit,
the strange experience of beauty;

its existence is too much;
it tears one to pieces
and each fresh wave of consciousness
is poison.

The detachment of Moore as watcher is not totally lost, but seems (by design) never fully recovered again in the poem. A woman's fine bitterness against the West's endless assault upon Eve is felt in Moore's description of the universal mother as "the central flaw" in the experiment of Eden, itself "an interesting impossibility" ecstatically described by Richard Baxter as "the choicest piece of my life." If Baxter's ecstasy (though not his eloquence) is qualified shrewdly by Moore's contextualizations, Eden is nowhere near so scaled down by her as is Adam, whose male pomp is altogether undermined. He is pretty well identified with Satan, and like Satan is: "alive with words, / vibrating like a cymbal / touched before it has been struck."

Moore's genius at her method allows her the joy of exemplifying her borrowings even as she employs them in a corrective polemic against male slanderings of women:

"Treading chasms
on the uncertain footing of a spear,"
forgetting that there is in woman
a quality of mind
which as an instinctive manifestation
is unsafe,
he goes on speaking
in a formal customary strain.

In the first quotation, Hazlitt is praising his precursor Edmund Burke for a paradoxically certain footing: for power, energy, truth set forth in the Sublime style. Burke is a chasm-treader, sure-footed as he edges near the abyss. But men less given to truth than Burke have very uncertain footing indeed, whether they forget or remember their characteristic brutalities in regard to a woman's "quality of mind." The poem's "he" therefore goes on speaking of marriage in Richard Baxter's ecstatic terms, as though marriage itself somehow could become "the saints' everlasting rest." Fatuously joyous, the male is ready to suffer the most exquisite passage in the poem, and perhaps in all of Moore:

> Plagued by the nightingale
> in the new leaves,
> with its silence—
> not its silence but its silences,
> he says of it:
> "It clothes me with a shirt of fire."
> "He dares not clap his hands
> to make it go on
> lest it should fly off;
> if he does nothing, it will sleep;
> if he cries out, it will not understand."
> Unnerved by the nightingale
> and dazzled by the apple,
> impelled by "the illusion of a fire
> effectual to extinguish fire,"
> compared with which
> the shining of the earth
> is but deformity—a fire
> "as high as deep
> as bright as broad
> as long as life itself,"
> he stumbles over marriage,
> "a very trivial object indeed"
> to have destroyed the attitude
> in which he stood—.

I hardly know of a more unnerving representation of the male fear and distrust of the female, uncannily combined with the male quandary of being obsessed with, fascinated by, not only the female but the enterprise of marriage as well. Moore imperishably catches the masterpiece of male emotive ambivalence towards the female, which is the male identification of woman and the taboo. Here the nightingale, perhaps by way of Keats's erotic allusions, becomes an emblem of the female, while the male speaker, ravished by the silences of the emblem, becomes Hercules suicidally aflame with the shirt of Nessus. The poor male, "unnerved by the nightingale / and dazzled by the apple," stumbles over the enterprise that is Adam's experiment, marriage:

> its fiddlehead ferns,
> lotus flowers, opuntias, white dromedaries,
> its hippopotamus—
> nose and mouth combined
> in one magnificent hopper—
> its snake and the potent apple.

We again receive what might be called Moore's Paradox: marriage, considered from either the male or female perspective, is a dreadful disaster, but as a poetic trope gorgeously shines forth its barbaric splendors. The male, quoting Trollope's *Barchester Towers*, returns us to the image of Hercules, and commends marriage "as a fine art, as an experiment, / a duty or as merely recreation." I myself will never get out of my memory Moore's subsequent deadpan definition of marriage as "the fight to be affectionate." With a fine impartiality, the poet has a vision of the agonists in this eternal dispute:

> The blue panther with black eyes,
> the basalt panther with blue eyes,
> entirely graceful—
> one must give them the path—.

But this mutual splendor abates quickly, and a rancorous humor emerges:

> He says, "What monarch would not blush
> to have a wife
> with hair like a shaving brush?"
> The fact of woman
> is "not the sound of the flute
> but very poison."
> She says, "Men are monopolists
> of 'stars, garters, buttons
> and other shining baubles'-
> —unfit to be the guardians

of another person's happiness."
He says, "These mummies
must be handled carefully—
'the crumbs from a lion's meal,
a couple of shins and the bit of an ear';
turn to the letter M
and you will find
that 'a wife is a coffin.'

This marvelous exchange of diatribes is weirdly stitched together from outrageously heterogeneous "sources," ranging from a parody of *The Rape of the Lock* (in which Moore herself took a hand) to a women's college president's denunciation of the male love of awards and medals on to a surprising misappropriation of a great moment in the prophet Amos, which is then juxtaposed to a brutal remark of Ezra Pound's. Amos associates the lion with Yahweh:

The lion hath roared, who will not fear? the Lord GOD hath spoken, who can but prophesy?
Thus saith the LORD; As the shepherd taketh out of the mouth of the lion two legs, or a piece of an ear; so shall the children of Israel be taken out that dwell in Samaria in the corner of a bed, and in Damascus in a couch.

Moore slyly revises the roaring prophet, making the lion every male, and the children of Israel every woman. Pound's dictum, that "a wife is a coffin" is presumably placed under the letter M for "male," and sorts well with Moore's unfair but strong revision of Amos, since the revision suggests that a wife is a corpse. In order to show that her revisionary zeal is savagely if suavely directed against both sexes (or rather their common frailties), Moore proceeds to dissect the narcissism of men and women alike, until she concludes with the most ironic of her visions in the poem:

"I am such a cow,
if I had a sorrow
I should feel it a long time;
I am not one of those

who have a great sorrow
in the morning
and a great joy at noon";

which says: "I have encountered it
among those unpretentious
protégés of wisdom,
where seeming to parade
as the debater and the Roman,
the statesmanship
of an archaic Daniel Webster
persists to their simplicity of temper
as the essence of the matter:

'Liberty and union
now and forever';

the Book on the writing table;
the hand in the breast pocket."

Webster, hardly unpretentious, and wise only in his political cunning, is indeed the message inscribed upon his statue: "Liberty and union / now and forever." As a judgment upon marriage, it would be a hilarious irony, if we did not wince so much under Moore's not wholly benign tutelage. That Book on the writing table, presumably the Bible, is precisely like Webster's hand in the breast pocket, an equivocal emblem, in this context, of the societal benediction upon marriage. Moore's own *The Waste Land*, "Marriage," may outlast Eliot's poem as a permanent vision of the West in its long, ironic decline.

Marianne Moore

Remembered as much for her black tricorner hat and cape as for her poetry, Marianne Craig Moore was an early Modernist and a quiet but forceful moralist. She was born in Kirkwood, Missouri, on November 15, 1887, to Mary Warner and John Milton Moore, a construction engineer and inventor. Moore's father was institutionalized prior to her birth; as a result, Moore never knew her father. However, the relationship between she, her mother, and her brother would prove to be the most powerful influence in both her life and her poetry. Moore grew up with religion as her mother kept house for her own father, John Riddle Warner, a Presbyterian pastor, in Kirkwood. After his death in 1894, Moore's mother moved the children to Carlisle, Pennsylvania, where Moore attended prep school. At 17, Moore matriculated into Bryn Mawr College, where she enjoyed great social success and began publishing her first poems and stories in its literary magazines, *Tipyn Bob* and *The Lantern*. She graduated with a BA in 1909 and enrolled in Carlisle Commercial College that same year, where she took secretarial courses for another year. She then taught at the U.S. Industrial Indian School at Carlisle until 1915, when she finally quit what she found to be an exhausting job. In the interim, her brother, Warner, with whom she was very close, had finished college and become a Presbyterian minister. The letters between all three family members were informative, instructive and intimate, often employing pet names and reviews of each other's activities and in the case of Marianne, her poems. She looked to her brother and particularly her mother to affirm the moral force of her poems, believing that art was meant to improve people's souls. In 1911, Moore and her mother traveled to Europe, taking in a number of art museums, fueling Moore's passion for the visual which often manifested itself in her very particular images.

1915 marked a watershed year for Moore; her poems were being accepted by some of the most promising new journals, *The Egoist*, *Poetry*, and *Others*. Moore also began to write critical essays and reviews. In 1916, the two women (Moore and her mother lived together until her mother's death) moved to New Jersey to keep house for Warner; in 1918, they made their move into New York City, where Moore worked as a secretary and tutor. In 1921, Moore's career began its ascent. H.D., editor of London's *The Egoist* and a early Modernist/Imagiste, and her lover, Winifred Ellerman (aka Bryher), collected Moore's poems, unbeknownst to her, and published them in England in a small volume entitled *Poems*. While working as a librarian at the Hudson Park Branch of the New York Public Library, Moore had her first North American volume published, *Observations*; the book contained all of the original 24 poems from *Poems*, plus 29 more. That same year of 1924, she won a $2000 award from *The Dial* for achievement in poetry. During this time, she also became close friends with T.S. Eliot, William Carlos Williams, Ezra Pound, and Wallace Stevens. Their powerful positive critique of her work helped to establish her ethos with an immediacy seldom shared by other poets.

In 1925, Moore became acting editor of *The Dial* in place of Scofield Thayer, whom she would eventually replace as editor in 1926. She edited for four years, during which time she published no poetry of her own; however, her unwavering aesthetic while working with the magazine reinforced many of her own creative principles that she later refined. The four years exhausted her, and when *The Dial* closed, she and her mother moved to Brooklyn in 1929, where Moore returned to a life of privacy, though certainly not anonymity as she was well-known for her wit, knowledge, and conversational savoir faire. After more than seven years of poetic silence, Moore began publishing again and won the Helen Haire Levinson award from *Poetry*. In 1937, she published *Selected Poems*, with an enthusiastic introduction by T.S. Eliot. It was met with a largely positive critical reception with particular admiration of her use of syllabic lines, subtle rhyme, careful observation, and moral force. Coupled with the Levinson award, she was becoming a national figure, although the book did not sell particularly well.

In the next ten years, Moore was again writing steadily, publishing *The Pangolin and Other Verse* in 1936, *What Are Years?*

in 1941, *Nevertheless* in 1944, and *Rock Crystal: A Christmas Tale* by Adalbert Stifter, which Moore and Elizabeth Mayer translated. That same year, Moore received a Guggenheim Fellowship. In 1947, Moore sustained the worse loss of her life when her mother died. As that part of her life ended, she was elected to the National Institute of Arts and Letters and started translating the *Fables Choisies, mises en vers*, for which she would eventually win France's Croix de Chevalier des Arts et Lettres award when the book appeared in 1954. She also began wearing the tricorner hat and cape for which she would become famous. In 1951, she brought out her *Collected Poems*, which won the Pulitzer Prize and the National Book Award in 1952. It also won the Bollingen Prize the next year. The book would bring to light one of Moore's alternately most fascinating and frustrating idiosyncracies as a writer—her revising. Poems would take drastically altered states throughout her career, "Poetry" being perhaps the most famous of these, when it changed from thirty-nine lines to a cryptic three, though the poem of thirty-nine lines was re-printed in the notes, elevating "Notes" to a section of importance generally known only to readers of Eliot. Always fond of riddles, Moore refused to insult her audience with "connectives." Moore also played with the organization of her books, leaving some poems out of particular editions and re-ordering others in ways which suggested different meanings; though some might have been displeased with the changes, none questioned the force of intent behind them. Moore pointedly began her *Collected Poems* with the comment, "Omissions are not accidents."

Through the fifties, she enjoyed her most prolific publishing years: *Predilections*, in 1955, *Like a Bulwark* in 1956, *O To Be a Dragon* in 1959, and *Tell Me, Tell Me*, in 1966, *Puss in Boots, Cinderella, and Sleeping Beauty* retold in 1963, *The Arctic Fox* in 1964, *A Talisman, Idiosyncracy and Technique*, and *Poetry and Criticism* in 1965 and *The Complete Poems of Marianne Moore* in 1967 for which she received the Edward MacDowell Medal and Poetry Society of America's Gold Medal. During these years, she also appeared in *Life* magazine, *The New York Times*, *The New Yorker*, and *Esquire*, where she was featured with other

"Unknockables" like Kate Smith, Joe Louis, and Jimmy Durante, all characters everybody loved. In 1966, after writing poems about baseball, Moore threw out the opening day ball at Yankee Stadium, a sinking slider that she had practiced for a week. By the end of the sixties and the early seventies, Moore's health was declining due to a series of strokes, the last of which killed her on February 5, 1972. Her legacy is vast. She served as friend and critic to many of the modernists, friend and mentor to the next generation of poets, Elizabeth Bishop among them, poetry's grande dame to the general public, and a ground-breaking modernist for generations to come.

CRITICAL ANALYSIS OF
"The Steeple-Jack"

"The Steeple-Jack" first appeared in *Poetry* in 1932, as part of a triptych entitled, "Part of a Novel, Part of a Poem, Part of a Play." Famous for her tinkering, Moore later split the three poems of the triptych, "The Steeple-Jack," "The Student," and "The Hero," in addition to revising the poems themselves. When "The Steeple-Jack" reappeared in her *Collected Poems*, it was shorter and one of its sister poems, "The Student" had been pulled from the collection altogether only to reappear in the revised *Collected Poems* of 1951. Moore published these poems after seven years of silence, during which time she worked as the editor of *The Dial* from 1925–1929 and moved both she and her mother from Manhattan to Brooklyn, where her mother remained until her death and Moore remained until 1965. The time as editor of *The Dial* only solidified Moore's commitment to bringing moral force to her poetry. Critics assert that her editorial work further bolstered her strong aesthetic sense even though that same work kept her from writing her own poetry. Others believe that Moore's life in Manhattan had overwhelmed her and left her without the solitude necessary to create her often interior poems. With the advent of this new work, Wallace Stevens, T.S. Eliot, and William Carlos Williams praised her as an inventive new voice, "a poet that matters."

"The Steeple-Jack" which was the poem to begin her *Collected Poems*, represents the 'novel' portion of the original triptych. It begins with an immediate reference to Albrecht Dürer, a German artist and engraver. While writing an editorial for a 1928 issue of *The Dial* on Dürer's exhibit at the New York Public Library, Moore familiarized herself with him through his correspondence and journals, and in that she stumbled on a reference he made to wanting to see a beached whale that was near his home. While Dürer attempted the trip to see the whale, he was unsuccessful. Still, Moore must have been attracted to this spirit of wanting to see and to know. Ultimately she began her poem with it:

Dürer would have seen a reason for living
   in a town like this, with eight stranded whales
to look at; with the sweet sea air coming into your house
on a fine day, from water etched
   with waves as formal as the scales
on a fish.

On the surface, the poem begins as a pleasant enough incarnation of a seaside town along the east coast. The breeze blows through open windows and even the fish are ordered, but, at the heart of the image, eight dying or perhaps dead whales remain, who will in their slow decay begin to taint that 'sweet sea air' with the smell of death. Moore also suggests with the prominent, initial placement of the whales that they are truly the reason for coming, to see these mammoth animals stilled, up close and out of their element. Perhaps too to see what happens as a living being makes its way into death. Moore presents this fascination, with her ordered lines, in a manner completely reasonable. The study of death is as much a reason for careful attention as the formally scaled fish. This stanza also sets up the poem's careful syllabics, which Moore only breaks to prove a point in the fourth and fifth stanzas. Readers can expect six lines with a syllabic count of eleven for the first line, ten for the second, fourteen for the third, eight for both the fourth and fifth, and three for the final line. This formal attention creates expectation and order for the reader, both of which soothe the reader into almost ignoring the signs of unrest present in the descriptions.

In the second stanza, Moore broadens her view to include the seagulls whose formal attention matches that of the poet. They fly in ones, twos and threes, circling the town clock. Their flight is beautiful and almost effortless, the only thing that betrays the work, or the possibility for inner discord is "a slight/ quiver of the body," or the way in which they "flock/mewing" where the sea begins to change color. They perch themselves where there is the unexpected. In the next stanza, Moore employs vibrant colors to vivify her picture with both words of color and the mental images of Dürer's pictures. Along the shore line, Moore places lobster pounds and fish nets to dry. Everything seems suspended waiting for something to happen.

The fourth stanza introduces the change:

> whirlwind fife-and-drum of the storm bends the salt
>   marsh grass, disturbs stars in the sky and the
> star on the steeple; it is a privilege to see so
> much confusion.

Suddenly, a storm is brewing that will change the placid, slow-moving town. The storm's "fife-and-drum" band rallies nature to a battle of sorts, one that will unsettle more than the seagulls who already sense its power. It 'disturbs' not only heavenly bodies but also the inextricably earthbound star atop the steeple and the rhythms of the poem, which have changed from the set pattern to an erratic jumble of syllabics.

The voice which comments on the privilege of viewing the chaos is suddenly changed too, from the voice of the travel guide to the voice of the distant audience member. As a disinterested viewer, a person outside of the potential destruction, as she is an objective viewer of the dying whales, Moore can delight in waiting for the drama that will ensue with the storm's arrival, after all, she has no stake in the chaos; her only appointment is to watch. In later versions of the poem, Moore continues the confusion with a proliferation of plants, a Rappaccini's Daughter sort of garden, mirroring the growing unease of the poem's predicament and the presence of a student, sitting out on a hill reading books "not-native." His is the first human presence to appear in the poem and he, like the narrator, seems out of place, a distant observer and yet still an integral part of the town because it must be seen from the outside. However, in the 1935 version, the steeple-jack is the first human presence, a man working to straighten the skewed star.

His red coat and spidery moves add to the sense of portent building in the poem. This stanza too has an erratic syllabic count, suggesting unrest as it did in the stanza before. When the steeple-jack releases "a rope down as a spider spins a thread;" he seems suddenly evil, as if he were setting a trap for potential victims. It also brings to mind other famous moments in American literary history, when Jonathan Edwards in "Sinners in the Hands of An Angry God" warns of sinners as spiders being suspended above the flames of hell, or the traditional association of scarlet with sin and temptation made famous by Nathaniel Hawthorne. Moore herself suggests that he might be a character in more than this poem, "he might be a part of a novel." This phrase suggests associative thinking while her next phrase warns readers to retain the feeling of having seen this character without the specific name. The sign that he has placed on the sidewalk names him C.J. Poole, certainly an appropriate name for a fellow in a seaside town. The sign is "in black and white; and one in red/ and white says//Danger." Perhaps the chaos comes before the storm as Moore so dramatically signals with her stanza break, beginning the next one starkly, with "Danger."

The church on which the steeple-jack is working gets thrown into relief as Moore juxtaposes danger with the picture of the church:

...The church portico has four fluted
    columns, each a single piece of stone, made
modester by white-wash. This would be a fit haven for
waifs, children, animals, prisoners,
    and presidents who have repaid
sin-driven

senators by not thinking about them....

The church becomes a place of duplicity, with its carefully white washed columns, meant to conceal their craftsmanship. It also figures as a halfway house to hide people without the means to protect themselves, reinforcing the notion of half-truths and disguise. In a satirical move, Moore includes among her disenfranchised the president; some critics have suggested that this line refers to Coolidge while others suggest it is a reference to Hoover.

The next stanza recounts the other buildings of the town, and claims that "The hero, the student,/ the steeple-jack, each in his way/is at home." Without the intervening stanzas and the accompanying poems, it is difficult to make sense of these three. In the missing stanzas, the student sits and views the town that is not his own and reads books that are "not-native," suggesting that his eye is that of the poet; the hero is one who asks the appropriate questions and does the appropriate things all without really interacting with the people with whom he is speaking, suggesting that his is a drama already written, in which he is only an actor going through the motions. The steeple-jack suggests the stories of other writers. Combined the three complete the title of the triptych, "Part of a Poem, Part of a Play, Part of a Novel."

The poem seems to place itself as the beginning of each potential work. It happens in the moment just prior to chaos when stories start themselves. Moore writes:

It scarcely could be dangerous to be living
    in a town like this, of simple people
who have a steeple-jack placing danger-signs by the church
when he is gilding the solid-
pointed star, which on a steeple
stands for hope.

Moore's phrasing, like many of her images, can be read in many ways, by the naïve as positive, by the cynical as negative and portentous. The steeple-jack uses danger signs but they are vague as to what constitutes the danger. Is it the false hope of the painted star that only has meaning once it is placed in the context of the steeple? Is it the danger of the church which through the course of the poem has been the sight of the devilish steeple-jack who works there alongside seemingly more benevolent powers? Or is it the continued disguise of the painted church, the painted star, both of which are crooked, or "not true," or the lack of people really looking at their landscape? Under the cover of a pleasant seaside picture, Moore enacts the claim of her poem, writing a piece more complex than its attractive images and smooth syllabics would suggest.

"The Steeple-Jack"

A. KINGSLEY WEATHERHEAD ON PERSPECTIVE

[A. Kingsley Weatherhead is Professor Emeritus of English at the University of Oregon and is the author of *The Edge of the Image* and *Stephen Spender and the Thirties*. In this excerpt, Weatherhead discusses the change of perspectives in the poem.]

The two kinds of vision may be easily recognized in "The Steeple-Jack," where an important contrast is formed between the images provided by the bird's-eye view of the town—the view enjoyed by the steeple-jack aloft—in the first part of the poem and those that come from a close study in the second. In the first four stanzas of the shortest version of the poem,[1] the emphasis on sight is apparent: there are "eight stranded whales / to look at"; "You can see a twenty-five- / pound lobster"; and the storm is visible: "… it is a privilege to see so / much confusion." But the view in this part of the poem provides less a description of a town than a description of a sentimental picture of one: water is "etched / with waves," gulls sail around the lighthouse, the sea is too richly tinted.

The storm destroys the romantic picture exactly as it does in Hawthorne's "Sights from a Steeple." In the fifth stanza, with the lines "A steeple-jack in red, has let / a rope down as a spider spins a thread;" the point of view changes, and the general view gives way to the close study. The act of seeing is now different; the words describing it are not now "You see," but "One sees," "one" being the pronoun the poet frequently uses for personal observations. The items now perceived are parts of the real everyday world, the schoolhouse, the post office, the fish- and hen-houses; they are not necessarily picturesque, but simply objects seen by a viewer with, literally and figuratively, her feet on the ground.

One important image purveyed by the accurate view is the

sign set up by the steeple-jack. Its message is given some prominence in the poem, appearing as the first word of a stanza: the sign

> in red
> and white says
>
> Danger....

We are warned not only of the physical danger but of the danger of sentimentally concluding that the town is merely the picturesque place that has been presented in the images mediated through the vision of the steeple-jack, which have occupied us up to this point. There follow the realistic details; and we deduce, among other things, that the livelihood of the town, depending as it does on the unpredictable sea, is more precarious than the birds-eye view had suggested:[2] the storm which had been a glorious sight had other implications. All the same, the final stanza begins, "It scarcely could be dangerous to be living / in a town like this" and concludes by describing the steeple-jack gilding the star which "stands for hope." The point is that when the danger has been fairly faced, as it has here by the acknowledgment of the realistic situation, it has been contained. The realistic view has neutralized the sentimental one; and from ground level looking up one may safely entertain hope—a hope based on solid foundations, as the star is based on the steeple of the church.

NOTES

1. Marianne Moore, *Collected Poems* (New York: Macmillan, 1959), pp. 13–14. Hereafter *CP*. In *Selected Poems* (New York: Macmillan, 1935) the poem has twelve stanzas. Hereafter *SP*. It was revised in 1961 and appears with thirteen stanzas in *A Marianne Moore Reader* (New York: Viking Press, 1965), pp. 3–5.

2. Louise Bogan, "Reading Contemporary Poetry," *College English*, XIV (February, 1953), 258. See also Marie Borroff, "Dramatic Structure in the Poetry of Marianne Moore," *The Literary Review*, II (Autumn, 1958), 112–23.

—A. Kingsley Weatherhead, "Marianne Moore." *The Edge of the Image: Marianne Moore, Williams Carlos Williams, and Some Other Poets* (Seattle: University of Washington Press, 1967): 59–61.

[Bonnie Costello is a Professor of English at Boston University. She has written several books of criticism: *Elizabeth Bishop: Questions of Mastery*, *Wallace Stevens: The Poetics of Modernism*, and *Marianne Moore: Imaginary Possessions*. In this essay, Costello discusses the impact of Dürer on the poem.]

If we look carefully at "The Steeple-Jack" we can see some of the ways its resident artist is effecting the presentation. Aside from the direct references to Dürer we notice his implied vision in the choice and treatment of detail. The water is "etched / with waves as formal as the scales / of a fish." The seagulls fly "one by one, in two's in three's." The wealth of detail is carefully measured, symmetrically balanced. The highly pictorial quality of the scene is heightened by color as well as shape, but again the stylization is emphasized both in the comparison of the scene to a water color by Dürer and in the balance of the seagulls with other birds (peacocks, guineas) present only metaphorically.[18] The emphasis on pictorial harmonies suggests that we are already looking at an idealized, not an actual, objective scene.

The pastoral world of this New England town (a little like Robert Lowell's Castine in "Skunk Hour") seems to be a microcosm of sorts, but the negative elements of the larger world have been absorbed and transformed by its overall serenity. The storm is a "whirlwind fife-and-drum"; the terrain sponsors a variety of flora and fauna, but the most exotic and most threatening elements have been displaced by milder surrogates. "You have the tropics at first hand," but a diminutive tropics of trumpet-vine and snapdragon, not banyans or frangipani. "The diffident little newt" substitutes for "exotic serpent life." (As with Dürer, Moore's robust enthusiasms for the particular led her to long, enchanting lists of flora and fauna which she canceled and then reinserted with her usual ambivalence toward such excess.)[19] It could not be dangerous to be living in a town like this, without the lures of destructive ambition; self-contained as it is, it seems the dream of the tourist, a heaven on earth where he can escape the harsher aspects of life. Or can he? Moore may be taking the lead from Dürer in planting apocalyptic symbols in everyday settings. Dürer would not have lived in a town like this to escape mortality, but to study and represent it. What could be more apocalyptic, more humbling than a vision of a stranded whale, though a conventional tourist might not see the meaning, and take it only as a natural wonder. The seagulls fly over the clock, again recalling our mortality. Danger is here, disturbing "stars in the sky and the / star on the steeple." It does not overwhelm the scene or violate its representational surface with its symbols, but rather creates a mild "confusion." The church spire has a quaint pitch which reminds us that it is "not true," both in the architect's and in the moralist's sense. The neat balance of the opening is offset by tremors. This town has the natural human tendency to pride and pretense, irony and self-deception, though its "four fluted / columns" are "made / modester by whitewash." Moore writes not in harsh judgment but as an observer, one who can both admire the setting and read the signs, who can see the flaws and compromises in this town which seems so prim. In this sense she identifies not only with Dürer but with "the student named Ambrose" (returned to the poem in 1961), who sees this world as someone who has gone beyond it, who appreciates its aesthetic "elegance" while he sees its moral limits.

NOTES

18. Isabel Cooper, "Wild Animal Painting in the Jungle," *Atlantic Monthly,* July 1924: Rosenbach 1250/5, 29–30.

19. A line was omitted, probably by accident, from *Collected Poems* and *Complete Poems.* It read: "the curve of whose diving no diver refutes. Upon spider-hands with."

—Bonnie Costello. *Imaginary Possessions* (Cambridge: Harvard University Press, 1981): 195–196.

[John M. Slatin teaches at the University of Texas. He is the author of *Savage's Romance*, a critical exploration of Marianne Moore's poetry. Here, he chronicles Hawthorne's influence on the poem.]

Just how dangerous the steeplejack really is begins to appear in the following passage from Harold Donald Eberleis' *Little Known England*, in which Eberleis quotes John Leland:

> ... there is the spire and choir of St. Alkmund's where "in the year 1533, upon Twelffe daye, in Shrowsburie, the Dyvyll appeared ... when the Preest was at High Masse, with great tempeste and darknesse, so that as he pasyd through, he mounted upp the Steeple in the sayd churche, tering the wyers of the clock, and put the prynt of his clawes upon the 4th bell, and tooke one of the pinnacles away with him, and for the Tyme stayde all the Bells in the churches within the sayd Towne, that they could neither toll nor ringe."[46]

This anecdote was transcribed from Moore's published notes to *What Are Years?* (1941), where it is used to account for a phrase in "Walking-Sticks and Paper-Weights and Water-Marks," a poem first published in November 1936. I have taken it from *What Are Years?* only for the sake of accuracy in transcription (Moore copied it into her reading diary in the fall of 1931, well before "The Steeple-Jack" was published) and use it here because this passage informs Moore's vision of the "man in scarlet," and identifies him as none other than "the Dyvyll."

In Leland's account, the devil climbs the steeple, just as the steeplejack does; more importantly, in Leland's narrative it is the devil himself who damages the steeple and brings on the "great tempeste." It is for this reason that I contended earlier that the storm, which in "The Steeple-Jack" precedes the appearance of the "man in scarlet" by a considerable margin, actually takes place in "cosmic" rather than "local" time, in a moment whose duration cannot be measured by the "town clock" because the devil has torn out its "wyers" and stopped its motion, as he has "stayde" the bells which might have warned us. Thus the storm only seems to precede the appearance of the "man in scarlet"; as in "The Fish," however, we have been shown the effects before being led to the cause.

It may appear that Hawthorne's "Sights from a Steeple," offered earlier as a possible source for Moore's steeplejack and for the "whirlwind fife-and-drum" of her storm, has now been disqualified. I am reluctant to dismiss it from consideration, however, not only because the poem is "luminous with *manifold* allusion"—in Emerson's phrase—but also because it seems to me that Hawthorne is entirely necessary to "The Steeple-Jack."

For in order to balance two such formidable antagonists as St. Ambrose and the devil, who are of necessity locked in permanent struggle, the poem requires yet another figure—a hidden one, capable of balancing good and evil in extremely complex situations, and of juxtaposing allegorical and literal interpretations of the "same" event or figure. This is what we have to do with the steeplejack, who "might be part of a novel" (so that Dürer cannot help us) but who is also a man with a name, part of the everyday world. Hawthorne, the author not only of "Sights from a Steeple" and "Rappaccini's Daughter" but also, and more importantly, of *The Scarlet Letter* (which is so nearly named in the lines that tell us how "a man in *scarlet lets* / down a rope as a spider spins a thread"), is entirely appropriate in such a role. He might indeed be "*part* of a novel."

The unobtrusive presence of Hawthorne—whom Moore somewhat grudgingly described as "a bear but great"[47]—explains much more than the steeplejack's shocking costume. One of the central episodes in *The Scarlet Letter* unfolds as the Reverend Arthur Dimmesdale, unacknowledged father of the child whose existence has made it necessary for Hester Prynne to wear the scarlet "A" on her bosom for seven agonizing years (the period of Moore's silence), delivers the Election Day sermon to a packed church. Hester stands outside with Pearl, listening intently though she is unable to make out the minister's words.

> Muffled as the sound was by its passage through the church-walls, Hester Prynne listened with such intentness, and sympathized so intimately, that the sermon had throughout a meaning for her,

entirely apart from the indistinguishable words.... Now she caught the low undertone, as of the wind sinking down to repose itself, then ascended with it, as it rose through progressive gradations of sweetness and power.... Still, if the auditor listened intently, and for the purpose, he could detect the same cry of pain. What was it? The complaint of a human heart, sorrow-laden, perchance guilty, telling its secret ... to the great heart of mankind...[48]

At the height of his career, Dimmesdale stands at the center of his theocratic community, knowingly submerging his corruption in his congregation's desire to interpret his physical weakness as a sign of his spiritual strength (when in fact the state of his soul is accurately imaged in his physical condition). Hester stands apart, as always, but her stillness, like Ambrose's, is only the sign of the deep "feeling" with which she listens while the pitch of Dimmesdale's voice reveals the sin he has never been able to confess openly. As she listens, her attitude resembles that of Moore's hero, who "doesn't like" "standing and listening where something / is hiding," but does it anyway—and what Hester hears is very much like what "The Hero" hears:

> The hero shrinks
> as what it is flies out on muffled wings, with twin yellow
> eyes—to and fro—
>
> with quavering water-whistle note, low,
>   high, in basso-falsetto chirps
>   until the skin creeps.

But the hero's shrinking is inward; it does not betray itself outwardly.

It may well be Hawthorne, too, who authorizes the introduction of "presidents" into "The Steeple-Jack." In "The Custom-House," the prefatory sketch affixed to *The Scarlet Letter*, Hawthorne details the story of his three-year career as a United States customs officer, a patronage post to which he was appointed by one president and from which he was turned out— "guillotined,"[49] as he rather chillingly puts it—by the next. Far from simply expressing his bitterness at having been removed from office, however, Hawthorne seizes the occasion to investigate the nature of the writer's relation to the state. He concludes that inasmuch as it was his dismissal from the moribund Custom-House which restored to him his life as a writer—for in the Custom-House his imagination had become "a tarnished mirror"—his abrupt "change of custom" has been for the best.[50] In thus accepting his forced retirement, Hawthorne makes himself "a citizen of somewhere else," a self-appointed and more than half-willing political exile like Hester Prynne, and he carefully points a number of analogies between himself and his character.

NOTES

46. Notes to *What Are Years?* (New York, 1941), 49; see also R1250/6, 35–36, for Moore's transcription from Eberleis. The entry was probably made in November 1931.

47. See Moore's review of the *Letters of Emily Dickinson*, in *Poetry* 41 (Jan. 1933): 223.

48. Hawthorne, *The Scarlet Letter*, Centenary Ed., 1:243.

49. Ibid., 41.

50. Ibid., 44.

—John M. Slatin. *The Savage's Romance* (State College: The Pennsylvania State University Press, 1986): 196–198.

BERNARD F. ENGEL ON "CONFUSION"

[Bernard F. Engel is the author of *Marianne Moore*. In this excerpt, Engel expounds on the use of 'confusion' in the poem.]

The "confusion" that exists in the seemingly placid environment of an ordinary town is examined in "The Steeple-Jack." The town, which represents the environment of most human lives, is calm seemingly, well ordered. Yet we remember that to be human is to face death—an inevitability Moore neither grows lyrical over like Whitman nor rages against like Dylan Thomas but accepts as part of reality. The first four stanzas, which picture the setting, open with the remark that the scene would have appealed to Albrecht Dürer, the German Renaissance artist. The reader is to recognize that Dürer is famed for placing apocalyptic visions in everyday settings. The poem presents the town on a "fine day" when there are "formal" waves on the water, an orderly flock of seagulls lazily circling the spires, water changing color in definite bands, and fishermen who have carefully spread their nets for drying. Yet this scene is not entirely tidy: on the beach are eight stranded whales (mention of an exact number adds to the impression of precision); the gulls, though steady, nevertheless quiver slightly; and, we are reminded, when storms come they put in disarray both grass and stars. (We may also recall that in one of her best-known poems, "A Grave," Moore has the sea function as a deceptive peril to man.) The words of the fourth stanza, "it is a privilege to see so / much confusion," sum up the appearance of the scene and the poet's attitude that a view of it is revelatory.

The last four stanzas present a specific example of the "confusion" noted in the town's general aspect and find a unity in the apparent variety. A steeple-jack in red, the color of warning, leaves a danger sign on the sidewalk while he gilds the star on a church spire. This little scene in itself constitutes one of the paradoxes of which Moore was fond. She delighted in such discoveries because they apparently pleased her in themselves and because they seemed to signify qualities inextricable from experience. She was most sure that she was presenting the nature of things not when she could give a clear—a simplified—explanation but when she could illustrate discontinuities. Belief in ultimate oneness was not to deny apparent diversities, what she termed "confusion." Quick statement of other details of the scene concludes that here the hero, the student, and the steeple-jack, "each in his way, / is at home." They are at home, we may assume, because this is a typical human community and these are types to be found among the "simple people" who live in it.

Yet perhaps these people are not merely simple. The last stanza opens with the seemingly casual, yet almost heavily ironic remark, "It could not be dangerous to be living / in a town like this," among people who have a steeple-jack place danger signs by a church while he gilds the steeple star that, the poet says, stands for hope. "Simple people" go about their business; they accept danger and hope as parts of life. Hope and danger, the poem seems to tell us, are inextricably mixed in life, are two primary qualities of it. This does not sadden the poet, for it is a "privilege" to see this mixture, the multitudinous and often paradoxical combinations of order and disorder, calm and storm, faith and doubt that make up our environment; it is exhilarating, her tone tells us. The attitude is that life is a mixture of possibilities that we would do well to face with an optimism that may be more than faint though it must be sensibly restrained.

Cuts from earlier versions eliminated four whole stanzas and portions of two others from the 1951 printing. The longer version reappears in 1981. The effect of the restored descriptive passages in this printing is to make the scene itself and the student Ambrose—mentioned here, though, as noted, also the subject of a now separate poem—serve as further instances of the paradoxes the poem presents. The lines detail the scene's mixture of northern and semitropical flora, the town apparently being one in a northern area warmed by an ocean current; the passage on the student remarks that he has a "not-native" hat and books, yet he likes the "elegance" that is native to the place.

—Bernard F. Engel. *Marianne Moore: Revised Edition* (Boston: Twayne Publishers, 1989): 23–24.

Robert Pinsky on the Poem as Embodiment of Moore's Relation to Community Life

[Robert Pinsky, former United States Poet Laureate, teaches at Boston University and is the poetry editor of *Slate* magazine. He is the author of many books of both poetry and criticism, for which he has won numerous awards. In this essay, Pinsky relates the poem to Moore's life in the community and society at large.]

The steeple-jack, the title figure in the first poem in Moore's *Complete Poems*, embodies the poet's relation to social or community life. He is not exactly isolated from the town: he serves the town by gilding its paramount symbol, and he also has posted two signs, one in black and white announcing his name and profession, and one in red and white that says "Danger." The steeple-jack is both prominent—he wears scarlet, he has a bold sign, he is high above—and also a small, attenuated figure, letting down his rope as a spider spins a thread. In his remoteness which is a measure of his courage, he resembles other figures, vulnerable and potentially lonely, who have in common their difference from the ambitious and gregarious. The stanza begins with the word "Danger," but the town offers relative safety for those who live with risk and rely on an inward reserve:

> This would be a fit haven for
> waifs, children, animals, prisoners,
> and presidents who have repaid
> sin driven
>
> senators by not thinking about them.

Relative safety is a governing ideal in Moore's haven. Those who are as Moore says "each in his way" at home here—the hero, the student, the steeple-jack—live familiarly with the risk of failure. They are at home with that risk, and with countervailing hope, and thus they strive, provisionally. Manners, compared to morals, are more or less by definition provisional, and "The Steeple-Jack" is a poem powerfully, subtly contrived to construct a model of the world of manners, our communal arrangement.

Here, the gap between Moore's personal utterance and the shared language of idiom serves to make the emotion all the stronger. In this secular world, the poet's voice mediates between the ordinary and the mysterious. It is a voice sometimes informal, yet never quite demotic; it is nonjudgmental, yet couched in the grammatical terms of the moralist: what "would be fit" or "is not right" or "what might seem" or "if you see fit." Her formal inventions bracket a capitalized "Danger" between stanza break and period, or stretch over line and stanza a phrase—"the pitch / of the church // spire, not true"—defining the boundary between secular imperfection and religious hope, or between the provisional and the absolute:

> Liking an elegance of which
> the source is not bravado, he knows by heart the antique
> sugar-bowl shaped summer-house of
>   interlacing slats, and the pitch
> of the church
>
> spire, not true, from which a man in scarlet lets
> down a rope as a spider spins a thread.

Because this figure puts out his danger-signs, "It could not be dangerous to be living / in a town like this." Up on the untrue spire gilding the solid-pointed star which on a steeple stands for hope, the steeple-jack is an artist at home in the town without being precisely in it. He leaves his laconic words of identification and warning behind, and puts the possibly deceptive gilding on the representation of a possibly justified communal hope. Though his very name, Poole, denotes a shared aggregate, and though he performs a communal service in a highly visible manner, he also embodies solitude and remove.

—Robert Pinsky. "Idiom and Idiosyncracy." *Marianne Moore: The Art of a Modernist*. Ed. Jay Parisi (Ann Arbor: The University of Michigan Press, 1990): 18–19.

GUY ROTELLA ON THE TREATMENT OF NATURE

[Guy Rotella is a Professor of English at Northeastern University. He is a poet and the editor of several scholarly books, *Reading and Writing Nature: The Poetry of Robert Frost, Wallace Stevens, Marianne Moore, and Elizabeth Bishop*, and *Critical Essays on James Merrill*. Here, Rotella expands on the way in which Moore uses nature in her poem.]

In "The Steeple-Jack," the "ideal" of nature controlled by civilization and art is significantly qualified. Culture is admired for its potent orderliness, but nature retains the power to threaten and destroy. At the same time, nature's ability to remain beyond the reach of our conceptions and contraptions grants pleasure and inspiration; the Fall seems not unfortunate. Moore's poem praises art and also exposes the threat that art will carry its proclivity for order too far: the sea's etched waves are overly simplified; "white and rigid" in their groove, the boats seem dead or fake. The rhyming of "the" and "sea" and "a" and "way" is strained. The artist Dürer presides over this poem, and rightly so: Moore shares his interest in both details and generalizations. As Moore would have done, he traveled far to see a stranded whale with his own eyes; he arrived too late, and much of his best work, again like hers, presents material already represented. In a process that Moore's rhyme approves, Dürer artistically "changed" what is to what is usefully "arranged." But Dürer, like Moore herself, could exceed what Moore could ratify. His "realistic" pictures are geometrical abstractions based on what he assumed are the objective absolutes of mathematical perspective. In consigning the town to him, Moore both praises and disclaims. He could see a reason for living in a town like this. She could, too, while seeing others for staying away.

"The Steeple-Jack" begins as an etching, then adds color to the scene, then people. The picture begins to move. As it does, it gathers social and political application. There are snakes and rats in lovely gardens; there is also human suffering and evil in this pristine place. A steeple-jack—perhaps he has been repairing storm damage (although, as if to further confuse our expectations, Moore says "he might be part of a novel")—lowers himself from the steeple of the church. He seems able; like an artist he "signs" his work, and he recognizes and warns his fellows of danger. But his scarlet garb and spidery movements have a devilish cast. Whatever the quality of the steeple-jack's work, "the pitch / of the church // spire [is] not true"—as the student named Ambrose insightfully knows. The church is white, but "pitch" defiles. Whether or not the steeple is "perpendicular," it is "not true" in some more metaphoric and essential sense, one it requires vision to perceive. Moore's response again accommodates. The church's whitewashed columns suggest both modesty and a whited sepulchre. "True" or not, the church is "fit haven" for those who deserve it: "waifs, children, animals"; it is perhaps even an apt sanctuary for "prisoners." But the church can also be a "front" to conceal the real motives of those who use piety and politeness as artful cultural screens to evade their moral and ethical duties—like the "presidents" who conveniently and decorously ignore "sin-driven // senators."

"The Steeple-Jack" manipulates the signs of art and nature and of form and danger in order to accommodate the contradictory human need for significant shapes that resist the flux of experience but that do not dominate and destroy it. Moore praises and condemns, but finally accepts, and perhaps forgives. Her conclusion—after asserting both with and without irony that "[i]t could not be dangerous to be living / in a town like this"—compares the artist to the steeple-jack. Each places "danger-signs by the church" while "gilding" the star on the steeple. We use art to decreate false constructs, to repair "untrue" creations, and to make "untrue" creations of our own. The greatest danger of all is that we will confuse the sign for substance or give up any hope of contact between sign and substance at all. Like art or social institutions, the star on the steeple "stands for hope." To stand for does not prove, and there are stars that stand for nothing. Gilding may be a guilty imposition. Yet hope is not undone. Moore ends "The Steeple-Jack" and other poems of the thirties as she said Stravinsky ends his compositions, "with the recoil of a good ski-jumper accepting a spill."[80] It figures human helplessness and skill, as if illusion revealed keeps illusion sustained.

NOTE

80. *Complete Prose* 324.

> —Guy Rotella. *Reading and Writing Nature: The Poetry of Robert Frost, Wallace Stevens, Marianne Moore, and Elizabeth Bishop* (Boston: Northeastern University Press, 1991): 181–182.

ROBIN G. SCHULZE ON MOORE'S AND WALLACE STEVENS'S PSYCHIC DISTANCE

[Robin G. Schulze is an Associate Professor of English at the Pennsylvania State University and the Director of

Undergraduate Studies. She is the author of *The Web of Friendship: Marianne Moore and Wallace Stevens,* and *Becoming Marianne Moore: The Early Poems, 1907–1924.* In this excerpt, Schulze compares the psychic distance of Stevens and Moore.]

To Stevens's mind, the "people" in the poem also serve the function of qualifying the poet's vision. As George Bornstein points out, Stevens often employs the provisionalizing tactic of a double consciousness in his mature lyrics.[11] Rather than present his own imaginative experience directly, Stevens often observes another, separate mind confronting the world. As Bornstein puts it, Stevens "refracts mental action of one mind through the apprehension of a second," distancing himself from the potentially oppressive ordering force in the poem.[12] As Stevens reads "The Steeple-Jack," Moore practices the same procedure; she does not view her fishing village directly, but through "the mask or mood" of Dürer, putting herself immediately at a remove from whatever ordered vision the poem has to offer. As Stevens points out, however, Dürer constitutes only one ordering force among many in Moore's poem and, tracing the nested visions of Moore's characters, Stevens revels in the multiplicity of her display:

> The people in the poem are Dürer;
>
>   The college student
> named Ambrose sits on the hill-side
>   with his not-native books and hat and sees boats
>
> at sea progress white and rigid as if in
>   a groove;

and C. J. Poole, Steeple-Jack, with one or two references to others. Poole is merely a sign on the sidewalk with his name on it. The last stanza is:—

> It could not be dangerous to be living
>   in a town like this, of simple people,

who have a steeple jack placing danger signs by the church
while he is gilding the solid-
          pointed star, which on a steeple
stands for hope.

(OP, 219)

As Stevens rightly notices, Moore does indeed fill her poem
with secondary consciousnesses. In "The Steeple-Jack," Moore
introduces Ambrose, her student and man of the mind, who,
under the influence of ideas "not-native" to his tiny and
somewhat self-satisfied village, shapes the landscape from the
panoramic perspective of a hilltop. Rather than order the vista
directly, Moore observes another mind in the act of ordering.
Ambrose's gaze arranges the boats in the harbor into a tidy,
"rigid" progression, but Moore removes herself from the
potential stasis of the act, viewing the arrangement only
indirectly. Moore repeats the tactic within the scope of
Ambrose's vision itself. "Liking the elegance of which / the
source is not bravado," Ambrose, Moore writes:

                              knows by heart the antique
sugar-bowl-shaped summer-house of
          interlacing slats, and the pitch
of the church

spire, not true, from which a man in scarlet lets
          down a rope as a spider spins a thread;
he might be part of a novel, but on the sidewalk a
sign says C. J. Poole, Steeple Jack,
          in black and white; and one in red
and white says

Danger.[13]

From his high vantage point, Ambrose sees the familiar shapes of
the village that he cares about enough to "know by heart." His
elevated perspective allows him to glimpse C. J. Poole, the
steeplejack in scarlet who, "placing danger signs by the church,"
gilds "the solid- / pointed star, which on a steeple / stands for
hope." Dressed in red, Poole and his craft embody the danger his

sign proclaims. A mark of the town's bravado, Poole's art reflects the needs of a community that places too much emphasis on the material manifestations of what should be powerful interior or imaginative sentiments. As Moore's line break in the final stanza proclaims, "gilding the solid," the steeplejack enacts Aaron's sin of substituting a prideful golden fixity for the mysterious idea of hope. Poole's art of beautiful surface runs the risk of distracting from the "startling inner light" that the star should bespeak. Moore's town is "not dangerous," however, because Poole's art, too, is provisionalized within the poem. Ambrose watches Poole at work in the same way that Moore observes Ambrose. Ambrose knows "by heart" that the pitch of the church steeple is "not true," and he is not seduced by Poole's, or the town's, errors of complacency. Nesting Poole's art within Ambrose's vision, Moore mitigates its spider's power to trap by placing it at two removes. For both Moore and Stevens, intellectual safety involves guarding against static symbols without substance.

NOTES

11. See Bornstein's discussion of Stevens's "Domination of Black," "The Idea of Order at Key West," "Connoisseur of Chaos," "The Sick Man," and "Landscape with Boat," in *Transformations of Romanticism*, 195–205.

12. Ibid., 198.

13. Marianne Moore, "The Steeple-Jack," part 1 of "Part of a Novel, Part of a Poem, Part of a Play," *Poetry* 40 (June 1932): 119–22. Moore reprinted "The Steeple-Jack" in *Selected Poems* (New York: Macmillan, 1935), 2–3. All further citations are to the version of the poem that appears in *Selected Poems* (hereafter cited as *SPMM*).

—Robin G. Schulze. *The Web of Friendship: Marianne Moore and Wallace Stevens* (Ann Arbor: University of Michigan Press, 1995): 110–112.

"The Fish"

Anthologists have long revered "The Fish," and though many critics agree that this is one of Moore's finest poems, their interpretations vary. Critics have taken this poem to represent beauty, the evils of war, an optical illusion, and a destruction of the traditional lyric self, to cite a few examples. Moore has made the task even more challenging with her infamous re-writes and her notebooks. In its original form as it appeared in a 1918 volume of *The Egoist*, Moore broke the poem into four-line stanzas with a syllabic count of 4, 8, 7, 8. In its subsequent incarnation in Alfred Kreymborg's *Others for 1919: An Anthology of the New Verse*, Moore changed it again to eight six-line stanzas with a syllabic count of 1, 3, 8, 6, 8. That version remained until her *Selected* in 1935 where it found its final form of eight five-line stanzas with a syllabic count of 1, 3, 9, 6, 8. These revisions changed the rhythm of the poem drastically, from a hasty move through the pictorial elements of the poem to a slow exploration that better served the fluid motion of the waters and the suggestion of the sublime, which lay within them.

Most immediately noticeable about the poem, even before reading, is the visual placement of the words on the page. They undulate as waves might, creating a visual rhythm to enter readers immediately into the watery world of the poem. Characteristically, Moore blends her title into the first line of the poem, again offering a kind of instant submersion, a directness that creates a tension with some of the more opaque elements of the poem. The emphasis on the visual continues in the images that Moore creates:

> The Fish
> wade
> through the black jade.
>   Of the crow-blue mussel-shells, one keeps
>   adjusting the ash-heaps;

opening and shutting itself like

an
injured fan.

Moore brings her way of knowing into the sea, likening the shapes to a menagerie of above water objects and beings. The juxtaposition often works to make the seemingly normal objects of the fan, the ash heap and the crow, doubly strange for existing where they were never meant. The use of particularly described color is also characteristic of Moore's absolute specificity of image, an attribute that linked her, perhaps erroneously, to the Imagist poets. Moore's word choice also merits particular attention as the "mussel-shells" described as "ash-heaps" and an "injured fan". In both cases, the word choice indicates something amiss, the remnants of a destroyed item, a fan somehow broken. Though the colors appear beautiful, the aabbc rhyme scheme fulfils formal expectations, and the sibilance of the lines is soothing to the ear, the choice of words belies all of these things. In the next stanzas, the images continue to accrue:

The barnacles which encrust the side
of the wave, cannot hide
        there for the submerged shafts of the

sun
split like spun
    glass, move themselves with spotlight swiftness
    into the crevices—
        in and out, illuminating

the
turquoise sea
    of bodies.

Again, objects not of the sea are made beautiful and foreign in this new landscape, and again, word choices indicate that there is something terrible also at work. All optical illusions, the barnacles encrust and hide, the sun becomes a search light forcing them from seeming havens, highlighting them against a sea of bodies, all shaded the same. Suddenly, the narrator cannot trust her own sight. Critic John Slatin suggests that this is the telling moment of the poem, where the writhing sea of bodies become those of World War I soldiers after a torpedo attack. For the less literal, it still imbues the lines with a strong sense of the sublime, the beautiful and the awful, co-existing as tensions in the sea, as the appearance of the outside objects suggest a similarly symbiotic relationship between the sea and land and sun.

In the next lines, "The water drives a wedge/of iron through the iron edge/of the cliff," making what seems invincible from the shore vulnerable to the water that slowly creeps into the structure, eventually destroying it almost from the inside out. In the wedge that the water creates, sea life flourishes in rich description: "whereupon the stars,//pink/rice-grains, ink-/bespattered jelly-fish, crabs like green/lilies, and submarine/toadstools, slide each on the other." Again, Moore brings shapes and associations from the shore into her description of the foreign seas. Still, it is here, that the poem begins to shift, away from the sea and its creatures to the cliff that resides within it. Moore's ultimate fascination with the cliff could be the articulation of many ideas. According to Margaret Holley, in an early draft of the poem, found on one of the Chatham worksheets, the lines read thus:

> The turquoise sea
> Of bodies.
> Sincerity of edge, in
> Such recesses of the mind, we
> Find flowers entwined
> With bodies there.

Moore wrote as notes in the side margin of this same draft "and/Found beauty intertwined/with tragedy." Such an overt commentary on the state of the mind would not have been Moore's style; instead, she relies on the images to tell the story, preferring not to insult her audience with too much information as she herself did not appreciate a clear through-line in a poem. The cliff might also be the sight of human destruction, made small by the awesome nature of the sea and the eventual thoroughness with which it will do its job. Or it may be the remnant of war, a battered reminder of things which can be both damaged and ultimately destroyed.

The sixth stanza begins with the focus clearly on the cliff:

All
external
    marks of abuse are present on this
    defiant edifice—
        all the physical features of

ac-
cident—lack
    of cornice, dynamite grooves, burns, and
    hatchet strokes, these things stand
        out on it; the chasm-side is
dead.

In this description, the cliff face is scarred by man in the many stages of his war-like development, from hatchets to dynamite. The side that endured the destruction is dead; mined clean of life, if not some other natural resource.

After all of this specificity, the poem retreats back into ambiguity with an inspecific pronoun referring back to a lost antecedent.

Repeated
    evidence has proved that it can live
    on what can not revive
        its youth. The sea grows old in it.

Presumably 'it' is the cliff, the defiant edifice. But what is it living on exactly and how is it that the sea can grow old within it? As in many poems, Moore leaves the reader to create a connective thread. If the cliff is living on the sea, and the sea grows old in the cliff, then it suggests a coupling of sorts, an uncomfortable and inevitable companionship, that will eventually lead to the destruction of one of the parties. It is a relationship not unlike that between man and nature as the defaced and defiant edifice shows; its wounds suggest a vulnerability that the rock face denies, begging the reader to question which will outlive the other, the human or the element of nature? Beyond that reading, the 'it' may indeed be a fish, the vessel in which the sea grows old, the body which needs the water to live although ultimately it is the water in which it will die.

"The Fish"

HUGH KENNER ON FORMAL DISTANCE AND THE SYNTHETIC VOICE

[Hugh Kenner is Professor Emeritus of English at the University of Georgia and the author of several books of literary criticism, with a particular interest in Joyce. In this essay, he discusses Moore's use of a synthetic voice and the way in which it creates a formal distance in the poem.]

Her poems are not for the voice; she senses this in herself reading them badly; in response to a question, she once said that she wrote them for people to look at. Moreover, one cannot imagine them handwritten; for as Ruskin's tree, on the page, exists in tension between arboreal process and the mind's serial inventory of arms, shields, tables, hands and hills, so Miss Moore's cats, her fish, her pangolins and ostriches exist on the page in tension between the mechanisms of print and the presence of a person behind those mechanisms. Handwriting flows with the voice, and here the voice is as synthetic as the cat, not something the elocutionist can modulate. The words on these pages are little regular blocks, set apart by spaces, that have been generated not by the voice but by the click of the keys and the ratcheting of the carriage.

The stanzas lie on the page, one after another, in little intricate grids of visual symmetry, the left margin indented according to complex rules which govern the setting of tabulator stops. The lines obey no rhythmic system the ear can apprehend; that there is a system we learn not by listening but by counting syllables, and we find that the words exist within a grid of numerical rules. Thus *The Fish* has 27 syllables per stanza, arranged in five lines on a three-part scheme of indentation, the syllables apportioned among the lines 1, 3, 9, 6, 8. And since a mosaic has no point of beginning, the poem is generated from somewhere just outside its own rigidly plotted field: generated not merely by ichthyological reality, but by two words, "The Fish," which are part of the first sentence but not part of the pattern, being in fact the poem's title. Therefore:

>   The Fish
> wade
> through black jade.
>
>   Of the crow-blue mussel-shells, one keeps
>   adjusting the ash-heaps;
>   opening and shutting itself like
> an
> injured fan.

To begin this sentence we read the title, and to end it we read three words (four syllables) of the next stanza: for the single stanza is a patterned zone specified within, but not coterminous with, the articulation of the sentences. The single stanza exhibits, in fact, an archaic disregard of the mere things human desire does with sentences. The voice shaping sentences is anxious to be understood; the stanzas are cut and laminated in severe corrective to that anxiety, posing against it their authority of number (1, 3, 9, 6, 8) and typography. They even invade the sounds of speech with their rhymes, not performing however the traditional offices of rhymes, not miming a symmetry, clinching an epigram, or caressing a melodic fluid, but cutting, cutting, cutting, with implacable arbitrariness: "like / an / injured fan."

It is a poem to see with the eye, conceived in a typewriter upon an 8-1/2" x 11" sheet of paper. If metric is a system of emphases, centered in human comfort, human hope, syllable-count is a system of zoning, implied by the objectivity of the words, which lie still side by side for their syllables to be counted. If the stanzas of "Go, lovely rose" are audible, created by the symmetries of the uttering voice, the stanzas of "The Fish" are visible wholly, created by the arrangement of words in typographical space, the poem made for us to look at. And it is amusing to notice that Miss Moore can revise a poem from beginning to end without changing a word in it. The first three times "The Fish" appeared in print its stanzaic system grouped the syllables not 1, 3, 9, 6, 8, but 1, 3, 8, 1, 6, 8, and in six lines, not five. What we have been looking at since 1930 is a revised version. The poem was twelve years old when the author made this change, and it is not, despite the mechanical ease of retyping with newly set tabulator stops, a trivial change, since it affects the system by which pattern intersects utterance, alters the points at which the intersections occur, provides a new grid of impediments to the overanxious voice, and modifies, moreover, the obtrusiveness of the system itself, the new version actually relents a little its self-sufficient arbitrariness, and consigns more leisurely fish to only half as many winking little quick monosyllabic turns. One can nearly say, putting the first and second versions side by side, that we have a *new* poem, arrived at in public, without changing a word, by applying a system of transformations to an existing poem. One remembers Charles Ives's statement that American music is *already written* (so that he had no need to invent tunes), and his pendant outburst on sound ("What has music to do with sound?"), as who should ask, what has poetry to do with people's anxiety to make themselves understood?

It contains, of course, the rituals generated by that anxiety, as music contains sound. Miss Moore's poems deal with those rituals as music dealt with them before the clavichord's mathematic was supplanted by the throb of the violin. She will not imitate the rising throbbing curve of emotion, but impede it and quick-freeze it. One impediment is the grid of counted formalisms. Another is the heavy system of nouns.

The Fish

wade
through black jade.

The black jade got onto the page by the same process as Ruskin's arms, shields and hills, but without benefit of the syntactic lubricants that slide us past a comparison: simile becomes optical pun. "Black jade" is an optical pun. So are the "ash-heaps" of the "crow-blue mussel-shells." Optical precision has brought these ash-heaps and crows into the poem; a moment later it will bring in a fan, to swell the bizarre submarine population; and before the poem is over we shall have taken stock of spun glass, turquoise, stars, pink rice grains, green lilies, toadstools, an iron wedge, a cornice. Each of these optical puns a moment's thought will assimilate; yet each such moment interrupts the attention (which simply does not expect to encounter such objects under water) and interrupts also the expected mechanisms of the English sentence, which has two places for nouns, before verbs and after them, actor-noun and patient-noun, "John threw the ball" but not "move themselves with *spotlight* swiftness." Miss Moore's sentences, unlike those of Olson or Creeley, are formally impeccable; but that impeccability, like the straightness of the horizontal lines of a graph, takes some searching out, interrupted as it so constantly is by repeated intersections with different systems entirely for dealing with nouns.

—Hugh Kenner. "The Experience of the Eye." *The Southern Review* 1 (October 1965).

TAFFY MARTIN ON MOORE'S RADICAL VIEW OF LANGUAGE

[Taffy Martin teaches at the University of Poitiers. She is the author of several critical articles works, *Marianne Moore: Subversive Modernist* among them. In this extract, Martin comments on Moore's radical view of language.]

The selective vision that Moore outlines here works well enough when her constructions are openly synthetic. In other poems, however, it is unsettling. In "The Fish," for instance, Moore employs a typically intricate stanzaic pattern along with evocative, sensual language to create a scene as unfathomable as it initially seems specific. The first three sentences are clear enough. The fish "wade through [the] black jade" of a sea where "submerged shafts of the // sun ... move themselves with spotlight swiftness" (CP, 32–33). Nevertheless, even within those sentences, Moore has hinted at the broken vision to follow. She describes the movement of one of the "crow-blue mussel-shells" with curious indirection. The movement of the sand helps a viewer to infer rather than to observe directly the broken movement of the shells. We know only that "one keeps / adjusting the ash heaps, / opening and shutting itself like // an / injured fan." The rest of the poem develops this hint of submerged movement and emphasizes its potential for violence: "The water drives a wedge / of iron through the iron edge / of the cliff" and the cliff itself shows "external / marks of abuse," both natural and deliberately inflicted. Having developed the apparent specificity of the poem to this point, Moore dissolves the scene in a flood of ambiguity. One side of the cliff provides a sheltered pool for sea life. In describing it, Moore begins a new stanza with a new sentence, a technique which, in her poems, often foretells dissolution.

> All
> external
>   marks of abuse are present on this
>   defiant edifice—
>   all the physical features of
>
> ac-
> cident—lack
>   of cornice, dynamite grooves, burns, and
>   hatchet strokes, these things stand
>   out on it; the chasm side is
>
> dead.
> Repeated
>   evidence has proved that it can live
>   on what it can not revive
>   its youth. The sea grows old in it. (32–33)

Contradiction dominates these images. "Lack of cornice," if it means a natural curve to the edge of the cliff, is certainly a physical feature of accident; but "dynamite grooves, burns, and / hatchet strokes" are just as surely not accidental. They are human interventions that "stand out" on the cliff. Thus, it should not be surprising that "the chasm side is dead." That announcement, however, makes the next two sentences entirely incomprehensible. If the chasm side is dead, ravaged as it clearly has been by the force of the water it contains, how does it live on the barnacles that adhere to its surface, on the shifting mussel shells that may or may not contain live mussels, and on the rest of the sliding mass of sea life that it shelters? Finally, why does the sea, clearly the most active and powerful force in this scene, grow old within this teeming shelter? Moore not only does not answer these questions, she does not even admit that she has asked them. The poem pretends that it works visually, whereas it should warn readers that images in poems are not always what they seem to be.

—Taffy Martin. *Marianne Moore: Subversive Modernist* (Austin: University of Texas Press, 1986): 94–95.

JOHN M. SLATIN ON "THE FISH" AS A WAR POEM

[John M. Slatin teaches at the University of Texas. He is the author of *Savage's Romance*, a critical exploration of Marianne Moore's poetry. Here, he suggests that the poem is really an anti-war statement.]

In the first version (1918), both the fish and the reader are impelled too quickly through the entire poem, as through the first sentence:

The Fish

Wade through black jade.

Here the primary emphasis falls on "jade," which concludes both the line and the sentence; the strong closure, enforced by punctuation and a heavy internal rhyme, creates a swift-paced line that belies the sluggishness of the movement in which we are being asked to believe. But when the same fish are made to

wade
through black jade

the new pattern slows their advance dramatically by isolating the verb, and so accentuates the great effort of their motion. With the verb singled out for attention, moreover, we become conscious of its oddity, for only creatures equipped with feet can wade: these "fish" are at least half-human—like the creatures of whom Moore was to write in "The Plumet Basilisk" (1933), they are "interchangeably man and fish."[37] The verb thus retains, and augments by extreme compression, the force of the simile by which the replacement troops had been discerned in "Reinforcements," "advancing like a school of fish through / still water." In "Reinforcements," "still water" is also clear water, as transparent as the simile itself; "black jade," however, is as opaque as the "black glass through which no light / Can filter" that forms the thick skin of the elephant in "Black Earth"— published only a few months before "The Fish." Having forced their way "through black jade," the all-too-human fish are lost from sight.

The reader, too, must now "wade / through black jade," stumbling over line-breaks as surprising in their placement as "still water" gone suddenly black and solid. Following the fish into the poem's stone sea, we find ourselves in a strange, ominously silent landscape filled with ruins. Amid scores of "crow blue mussel-shells" one moves, "adjusting the ash-heaps" to reveal that these are not living creatures but piles of empty, burned husks; and the lone survivor is weak, feebly "opening and shutting itself like / an / injured fan." Again the pattern does its work: by forcing the new stanza to begin on an insignificant word, it shifts emphasis to the second line, where because the fan is "injured" rather than torn or *damaged*, the line nags us once more with the faint, disturbing sense of a human presence, of a frail, crumpled body.

Although all seems quiet, the scene is still fraught with danger: barnacles looking for a place to hide "encrust the side" of a (solid) wave, but find no security. (The original version, which tells us that these "barnacles" are "trained to hide / There," hints that they, too, are human.) The sun's rays, refracted and "split like spun / glass" as they pass through the hard surface of the water, are themselves solidified: they become "submerged shafts," stabbing into the sea "with spotlight swift- / ness," probing (as the lineation suggests their quick, unpleasantly arhythmic motion) "into the crevices." No place is safe, and neither are we: when the searching light transmutes the sea from "black jade" to another stone, "turquoise," the syllabic pattern holds the image for a split second—just long enough for us to become conscious of a gentler, more soothing beauty—before allowing the light-change to reveal, with terrible deliberateness, that we are moving in a "sea / of bodies."[38]

The poem now arrives, quite literally, at its crisis: pressing relentlessly forward in the present tense, it turns *back*, chronologically, to discover the violence which has brought these bodies here. The "submerged shafts of the / sun," moving like spotlights, have found a target; and with sudden explosive force, "The water drives a / wedge / of iron through the iron edge / of the cliff."[39] (Wedges in Moore's poems are always weapons, and like the one that "might have split the firmament," they always possess tremendous explosive force.[40]) Just so, a submarine's spotlight finds its target, and a torpedo is driven through the iron hull of a ship, which looms clifflike above the surface. The concussion throws the undersea world into chaos:

> ... the stars,
> pink
> rice grains, ink
> bespattered jelly-fish, crabs like
>   green
>   lilies and submarine
> toadstools, slide each on the other.

Seemingly oblivious to such massive destruction, the stanzaic pattern isolates two splotches of bright color, pink and green, highlighted against the at-first-black and now turquoise sea, while the blasted troopship, scarred with "All / external / marks of abuse ... all the physical features" of an "ac- / cident" which is no accident but an act of war, settles to the bottom. There it rests, a "defiant edifice" with a gaping "chasm" in its "dead" "side."

The "submarine" world into which the poem has taken us,

then, is what Moore calls in "A Graveyard" "a well excavated grave," and "The Fish" is a bitterly elegiac poem mourning a loss which it is as helpless to restore as it has been helpless to prevent. But it *can* register the poet's guilt and horror at her troubled discovery of what a note in the margin of an early draft called "beauty intertwined with tragedy,"[41] and it *can* register the loss. "Dead" though it is, "the chasm side" lives "on what cannot revive / its youth"—on a poem which records and perpetually re-enacts its destruction, and which in doing so takes responsibility for it, although it can "revive" neither the "youth" of the ship nor the "youth" who went down with it. The poem can only note, with something like despair, that the sea filling the ship's hold "grows old in it."

NOTES

37. *Hound and Horn* 7 (Oct.–Dec. 1933): 32; *CP*, 23. As Pamela White Hadas points out in *Marianne Moore: Poet of Affection* (Syracuse, 1977), the phrase first appeared in Moore's poem "Ennui," published in the Bryn Mawr student magazine *Tipyn O'Bob* in 1909 (Hadas, 137–38).

38. Compare Williams's "The Yachts" (1935): Moore's influence shows itself near the end of the poem, where suddenly "It is a sea of faces about them in agony, in despair / until the horror of the race dawns staggering the mind; / the whole sea become an entanglement of watery bodies..." (Williams, *Selected Poems*, ed. Randall Jarrell [New York, 1963], 72).

39. In the MS and in the first published version of "The Fish," only the "wedge" was made of "iron"; the "edge / Of the cliff" was simply that. The change is crucial, for it reinforces the suggestion that we have to do with something other than "the natural object" here, and it establishes an equivalence between the destroying object and the object being destroyed.

40. See "In This Age of Hard Trying Nonchalance Is Good And—," in *Others: An Anthology of the New Verse* (1917), 79; and "Radical," *Others* 5 (Mar. 1919): 15.

41. MS of "The Fish," Rosenbach Archive.

—John M. Slatin. *The Savage's Romance* (State College: The Pennsylvania State UP, 1986): 73–75.

Margaret Holley on Catalogue and Spatial Ordering in the Early New York Poems

[Margaret Holley is the Director of the Creative Writing Program at Bryn Mawr College. She is a critic and a well-published poet. In this portion, she places the poem in the context of Moore's other early New York poems in terms of its techniques.]

Moore's gravitation toward more objective materials and presentations is perhaps most evident in the appearance of the catalogue as a central feature of the Chatham and early New York poems. The earlier verses "A Jelly-Fish" and "To a Chameleon" were focused on one subject, whereas "The Fish" is a plural title, and the fish are the first of many things being compiled, one after another, into a composite picture. About half of the poems of this period incorporate lists of objects, persons, behaviors, or quotations. This exercise in extended parataxis, that is, in placing items side by side, one after the other, rather than in the dominating and subordinating relations of hypotaxis, is a direct reflection of Moore's new orientation toward value. The avoidance of hierarchy as a structural principle bespeaks her new preference for a report rather than a verdict.

Even in the pieces that consist almost entirely of catalogue, Moore's new sense of the plenitude of the world is rarely allowed to expand her poems into Whitmanesque inclusiveness. Diversity as an image for universality appears in "People's Surroundings" and "An Octopus," but there and elsewhere the principle of selection is always visibly at work. Thus Moore's procedure is only apparently inductive, for inspection will reveal either a notion or a rhythm underlying the make-up of the list.

We have seen the pattern of antithetical metaphors that informs "Those Various Scalpels"; and "The Fish," published in the following year, is a carefully arranged meeting of opposites. An early draft and marginal note on one of the Chatham worksheets for this poem suggests the kind of ideas that were guiding its composition.[23] Originally arranged without stanza breaks, with each alternate line rhyming its first and last syllable, the early version contains about midway through it the following lines of thought on

> The turquoise sea
> Of bodies.
> Sincerity of edge, in
> Such recesses of the mind, we
> Find flowers entwined
> With bodies there.

In the margin of this passage about the mind, Moore has then pencilled in a further stage of thought:

> and
> Find beauty intertwined
>   with tragedy.

In its final version the poem's catalogue begins with flowerlike objects of beauty—

>   the stars,
>   pink
>   rice-grains, ink-
>   bespattered jelly-fish, crabs like green
>   lilies, and submarine
>   toadstools

—and closes with the "defiant edifice" of the cliff, the implacable and wounded stuff of tragedy with

> all the physical features of

ac-
cident—lack
    of cornice, dynamite grooves, burns, and
    hatchet strokes.

But the tentative lines have been omitted that would have turned these things into an allegory of the mind or of beauty and tragedy. The objects are observed speaking for themselves. The poem is the water, with its colored delicacies and their verbs of motion, that "drives a wedge / of iron through the iron edge / of the cliff"; and while we may allegorize the subject, the poet has refrained from doing so.

"The Fish" is also a good illustration of the enlivening challenge that the plenitude of this period presents to the spatial imagination. The motion of the mussel-shells, starfish, jelly-fish, and crabs in the first part of the poem is not so much a narration of action in time as it is a description of characteristic and repeated movement: "one keeps / adjusting the ash-heaps," keeps opening and shutting, moving and sliding. We are still being offered a scene rather than an event. Likewise in "Dock Rats," the ongoing scenic movement is carried by the present participle, that adjectival verb qualifying a noun: the river "twinkling like a chopped sea," "the tug ... dipping and pushing," and "the sea, moving the bulk- / head with its horse strength." These adjectival verbs add a certain element of movement to the spatial mode of perception. In the four middle stanzas on the sights of shipping, the main verb is always the simply listing copula "is ... is ... There is ... There is." And yet Moore's arresting catalogue of ships gains a sense of muscular activity from the adjectival verbs that fill it—the "battleship like the two- / thirds submerged section of an iceberg"; the "steam yacht, lying / like a new made arrow on the stream"; the "ferry-boat—a head assigned, one to each compartment, making / a row of chessmen set for play."

NOTE

23. Typescript of "The Fish" marked "Chatham, New Jersey, U.S.A.," Rosenbach.

—Margaret Holley. *The Poetry of Marianne Moore: A Study in Voice and Value* (Cambridge: Cambridge University Press, 1987): 61–63.

CRISTANNE MILLER ON MOORE'S RHYTHM AND SYNTAX

[Cristanne Miller is Chair of the English Department and Coordinator of the American Studies Program at Pomona College. She is the author of *Emily Dickinson: A Poet's Grammar* and *Marianne Moore: Questions of Authority* and co-editor of several books of criticism. Here, Miller analyzes Moore's rhythm and syntax.]

In Moore's poetry, syntax or phrasing, and hence any sense or "voice" or form as an extension of the physical body (Whitman's revolutionary version of organicism), functions in tension with lineation and stanza form rather than in harmony with them. James Scully notes that writers "attempt to solve those problems they have set for themselves, but set in concert with their historical circumstances, social values, class outlook, jobs, and the innumerable opaque or transparent 'aesthetic' and 'extra-aesthetic' encouragements and discouragements visited on them"; a poem is the "site of an exchange" between the "poetic" and "extra-poetic."[28] The tension between illocutionary and other language structures in Moore's verse strongly marks that she has "assume[d] responsibility for" the structure and "social transaction" of her text ("Line Break," 100). In an era of modernist nearly wholesale adoption of the free verse line as a "natural" basis for poetry, Moore's complex rhyming and syllabic stanzas proclaim her double oppositionality in asserting formal limitation as integral to her poetic.[29]

While illocutionary structures, not rhythms of speech, most distinctly mark Moore's poetry as spoken, poetic conventions of meter and rhyme most distinctly mark it as constructed, in spite of Moore's radical experimentation in constructing "naturalistic effects" in and through such forms. One might look, for example, at Moore's much-anthologized "The Fish." The last three stanzas read:

All
external
  marks of abuse are present on
    this
      defiant edifice—
  all the physical features of

ac-
cident—lack
  of cornice, dynamite grooves, burns
    and
      hatchet strokes, these things stand
  out on it; the chasm side is

dead.
Repeated
  evidence has proved that it can
    live
      on what cannot revive
  its youth. The sea grows old in it.

                    (P, 15)

Here no stanza and no line is syntactically self-contained; every sentence, every major phrase, and even some words are enjambed. The syllabic count of 1, 3, 8, 1, 6, 8 bears no organic relation to the poem's words, although one might imagine an impressionistic wave-like movement between short and longer lines. The stanza pattern also uses its limitations playfully—as in Moore's dividing the word "ac- / cident" mid-syllable. The poet's craft reveals itself in precisely this play, in her ability to place words appropriately within the severe limits of such a logically unpredictable form—for example, giving "defiant edifice" a line of its own; suspending the sentence-concluding adjective "dead" across a stanza break; or, earlier, dividing the alliteratively lovely phrase "sun, / split like spun / glass" among three lines to slow the readers movement through it. And this crafted enjambment of the syntax against the abstract grid of syllables indicates how fundamentally arbitrary that grid is.[30] Playing counted syllables against syntax depends on a process of reading, not hearing, the poem. Moore did write exclusively free verse for a few years during the twenties, but then returned to syllabic stanzas for her next forty years of writing.[31]

Like Moore's stanzas, her rhyme highlights the craft of her poetry and the static conventionality of verse in which rhyme sounds occur with a regularity that might be mistaken for natural. In a brilliant use and parody of this convention, rhyme occurs with visual regularity in much of Moore's verse but, because of the uneven line lengths of a syllabic stanza, *varying lapses of time and stress occur between rhyme sounds and hence the ear does not know when to anticipate the end of a line, or a rhyme: it might be after one syllable or after twenty-eight.* Moreover, because her lines are as apt to end with a function word (or, before the 1940s, even mid-word) as with the conclusion of a phrase or the kind of substantive monosyllable creating the "masculine" rhyme most valued in traditional prosody, Moore's end-rhymes are often syntactically unstressed. As I note in the concluding "cower/tower" rhyme of "Blessed Is the Man," Moore may also pun on conventional terminology for rhyme as either masculine (strong, full, perfect) or feminine (unstressed, polysyllabic, weak) through her typical reliance on "feminine" rhymes in combination with obviously artificial constructions of "masculine" rhyme or with particular placements of such rhymes. For example, returning to "The Fish," the technically masculine rhyme of "ac-" and "lack" calls attention to the wrenching of the word necessary to fulfill this convention. The mixed rhymes of "all / extern*al*" and "dead. / Repeat*ed*" are more typical of Moore's rhyme combinations of all styles and classes of words. Moore is also one of the great experimenters with rhyme in English, rhyming monosyllables with mid-word syllables, and creating a variety of consonantal, homophonic, sight, and two-syllable rhymes. Because her rhymes often occur within lines or line-internally between lines, Moore's (grammatically and aurally unaccented) end-rhymes receive even less relative stress. One hears the syncopation of sound and word repetition, but one is more apt to note the patterns of Moore's rhyming visually than aurally.[32] With both rhyme and syllabic stanza patterning, Moore uses a traditional form paradoxically to minimize the sense of regularity or tradition in her verse—and, again, thereby doubly emphasizing the constructed quality of her verse.

NOTES

28. "Line Break," in Robert Frank and Henry Sayre's *The Line in Postmodern Poetry* (University of Illinois Press, 1988), 98, 102.

29. See Leavell for the sequence of Moore's development of her stanza and rhyme structures in relation to other visual and poetic modernist experimentation with form, and for an excellent analysis of her stanzaic forms (*Prismatic Color*, chap. 2). Marie Borroff, in a comparison of the "layout" of Williams's and Moore's poems, attends to "enjambment, syntactically necessitated pauses, punctuation or the lack of punctuation, left-margin justification, indentation or lack of indentation, the spacing out of stanzas, the narrowness or width of the poem as laid out on the page, syllable-counts, rhymes ... [and] other visual and aural prosodic features" ("Questions of Design in William Carlos Williams and Marianne Moore," in the *William Carlos Williams Review* 14, no. 1 [Spring 1988]: 106). Borroff claims that Moore tends to use such features to slow rather than speed a readers progress through a poem. Rather than creating the momentum common in Williams's poetry, Moore makes one aware of "the constraints of form" and the liberatory potential of such constraint (110).

30. Paradoxically, this tension between line and phrase in some ways calls more attention to a prose rhythm in her poetry than do her free verse poems, with their coincident line and phrase structures. The tension between line endings and phrasal units in Moore's syllabic verse keeps the readers ear alert to the driving rhythms of the syntax as they forge through the lines.

31. As Holley writes, this experiment with the "free" form began with Moore's revision of a number of syllabic-verse poems into free verse lines. When she returned to writing poetry in the 1930s, she showed no interest in continuing her experimentation with the free verse line (PMM, 47–51).

32. Moore in fact typically marks her end-rhymes visually by indenting rhyming lines the same number of spaces from the left-hand margin—that is, she marks an aural practice with visual structures.

—Cristanne Miller. *Marianne Moore: Questions of Authority* (Cambridge: Harvard University Press, 1995): 74–77.

KIRSTIN HOTELLING ZONA ON MOORE'S DESTRUCTION OF THE 'STATIC LYRIC I'

[Kirstin Hotelling Zona is an Assistant Professor of English at Illinois State University. She is the author of *Marianne Moore, Elizabeth Bishop, and May Swenson: The Feminist Poetics of Self-Restraint*, and the editor of *Dear Elizabeth: Five Poems and Three Letters to Elizabeth Bishop*. In this essay, Zona discusses Moore's destruction of the 'static lyric I' as a feminist statement.]

Haraway is instructive when it comes to Moore's poetry because she makes clear the potential of partiality, the possibilities of the particular. Moore's "messages," in other words, are contingent upon her method: "We do not seek partiality for its own sake, but for the sake of the connections and unexpected openings situated knowledges make possible."[36] I cannot think of a more apt theoretical paradigm for the workings of Moore's poetic. Her sentences and stanzas, like the sea creatures in "The Fish," "slide each on the other,"

> with spotlight swift-
> > ness
> > into the crevices—
> in and out, illuminating

the limits to which we are accustomed by repeatedly citing and then blurring them, creating bridges out of boundaries.[37] What at first seems a "defiant edifice," the limit of one's understanding carved out by human "burns and hatchet strokes," is shown to harbor teeming life, a "sea" of sensibilities that has in turn transformed the edifice that may seem "dead":

> Repeated
> evidence has proved that it can
> > live
> > on what cannot revive
> its youth.
>
> > > *(Poems,* 15)

By recalling Foucault's explication of knowledge as produced rather than foreclosed by prohibition, we may better understand Moore's "edifice," the "chasm side" (*Poems*, 15) of which seems dead, as the shape of our assumptions.[38] Apparently static and immovable, "defiant" in its authority, the lifeless edifice appears to both predate and outlive the sea; in its very inorganicness it seems to claim omniscience and thus a kind of a priori realness. But the incessant, wavelike motion of the poem disrupts this vision of impermeability, as Moore's highly constructed "edifice" is seen to embrace the sea, which "grows old in it" (15). Collapsing the distance between title and poem, beginning and end, the rippling stanzas *become* the wave of the poem, driving a

> wedge
> of iron through the iron edge
> of the cliff, whereupon the stars,
>
> pink
> rice grains, ink-
> bespattered jelly-fish, crabs like
> green
> lilies and submarine
> toadstools, slide each on the other.
>
> (15)

The tide of the poem, the motion of the speaker's vision, erodes the stability of the edifice by introducing, then interlacing, the particularities of its inhabitants. Consequently, the "defiance" of the edifice becomes a life-giving embrace. The juxtaposition of rocklike cliff and life-drenched sea is confounded as each becomes the agent of the other. Importantly, the sea "cannot revive" the cliff's "youth," and vice versa—innocence is lost in the wake of unfinished, as opposed to ontological, meaning. No lyric "I" transcends this poem, and as we come to understand the cliff's mutability, we also learn that Moore's "objective," partial vision is most promising in its exposure of our own.

It is crucial to focus on the transformative potential of Moore's partiality and situated knowledge because this method of observation has been misunderstood as apolitical, superficial, or distancing. Various readers, feminist and otherwise, have interpreted Moore's observational verse as deflective, with its dazzling surface sheen warding off connection. Echoed by Moore's eclectic vocabulary, weblike network of notes and quotations, unconventional rhymes, midword enjambments, and fastidious manipulations of form, this characteristic has seemed to many the hallmark of a self-protective distancing. Moore, however, is after just the opposite. By offering a remarkably precise vision of her surroundings and a concomitant ungrounding of the "I" that frames the environment, she proffers poetry as an ongoing process in which meaning is made through interaction with an audience, rather than simply presented. (In this light perhaps we can better understand Moore's almost unmatched dedication to revision.) Just as Moore's poems displace the static lyric "I," so they reveal the extent to which the poet is implicated by her strategy of selfhood. Moore's poems are often followed with notes that, unlike Eliot's, do not direct the reader to a fuller understanding of the poem by way of broader contextualization, but rather point one outward, toward an ever widening pool of associations that may or may not add discernible "meanings" to the poem. In this case the poem emerges as a starting point, an occasion for interaction with the world around us, rather than a conclusion garnered from the roamings of a poet's "I."

NOTES

36. Haraway, *Simians, Cyborgs, & Women*, 196.

37. "The Fish" (*Poems*, 14–15). I read from this version rather than the slightly revised *CP* version (32) because the fluid stanzaic form of the earlier draft more clearly adduces the connection between poem and sea. First published in the *Egoist* 5 (August 1918): 95.

38. See Michel Foucault's "Repressive Hypothesis," in *The History of Sexuality*, vol. 1, *An Introduction* (New York: Vintage Books, 1980), part 2.

—Kirstin Hotelling Zona. *Marianne Moore, Elizabeth Bishop, and May Swenson: The Feminist Poetics of Self-Restraint* (Ann Arbor: The University of Michigan Press, 2002): 22–24.

CRITICAL ANALYSIS OF

"Poetry"

"Poetry" is perhaps one of the most confounding revisions of the Modernist era. The poem changed from a well-rounded thirty-eight or thirty-nine lines to an anorexic three with multiple incarnations in between. When the final cut version made it into the *Collected Poems* of 1967, critics and long-time readers felt betrayed. Critic Grace Schulman exclaimed, *"Three lines?"* and poet-critic Anthony Hecht mourned the loss, feeling that as a long time reader and lover of the poems he should have some say in what remains. Apparently, Moore herself couldn't quite bear to part with the longer version as the poem, in its thirty-nine line glory, as it appeared in the notes of the book, thereby elevating notes to a status of near poetry. The inclusion in the notes may, indeed, have been ironic, a little witticism on the part of Moore, who claims in her poem that even "business documents and school-books should not be discriminated against." Perhaps Moore meant to add notes to the list of possible sites for poetic happenstance. This critique will look at the version as it appears in the "Notes" of the 1967 *Collected Poems*.

The poem begins with a conversational appeal to the audience and an immediate literary reference, a popular device of Moore's.

> I, too, dislike it: there are things that are important beyond all this fiddle.
> Reading it, however, with a perfect contempt for it, one discovers in
> it, after all, a place for the genuine.

Readers feel, from the beginning, the intimacy created by confession, one that is perhaps a little sly, a small rhetorical bridge that the poet waits for the reader to cross that she might better draw him/her in for a refutation of her initial claim. The reference, the first of thirty-some, is to *The Notebooks of Samuel Butler*, Butler recorded his conversation with a young boy wherein the boy claims to dislike poetry. With the literary referent, Moore also draws in the presumably well-read audience of fellow poets and critics. Within three lines, she has made invitation to both the lay people and her peers. She also references "this fiddle"—the insincere fiddling to make poems better without the starting point of what she calls the genuine.

These three lines set forth her notion of the genuine, and they too spring as much from the author's mind as from a quote that she copied from an issue of *The Spectator* of May 10, 1913. In the quote, a reviewer seeks to explain why G.B. Grundy's *Ancient Gems in Modern Settings* still interests him. He claims that "All appeal to emotions which endure for all time, and which, it has been aptly said, are the true raw material of poetry." Moore clearly believed that good poetry contained some timeless appeal, some truth as per "the genuine." It suggests that however much Moore loved her verbal high jinx and extensive, Latinate vocabulary, she firmly held that it must be in service of something greater.

Moore begins to move into the first action of the poem:

> Hands that can grasp, eyes
> that can dilate, hair that can rise
>   if it must, these things are important not because a
>
> high-sounding interpretation can be put upon them but because they are
>   useful.

The actions suggest response and engagement, signals of the genuine at work. They are useful because they are real and active, regardless of whatever high-minded explication someone wants to give them. They are signifiers of the engaged audience, one that might act. In the next lines, Moore warns against

> ...when they become so derivative as to become unintelligible,
> the same thing may be said for all of us, that we
> do not admire what
> we cannot understand:

Poems, words, phrases that become so common that people fail to respond to them become dead, even resented by the audience. Because they fail to connect after so much use and manipulation, as readers and human beings, we no longer admire the poet who uses the instinctive phrase, we come instead to resent it. Moore then lists other sights that we cannot understand or admire:

                                    the bat
        holding on upside down or in quest of something to

    eat, elephants pushing, a wild horse taking a roll, a tireless wolf under
        a tree, the immoveable critic twitching his skin like a horse that feels a flea,
        the base-
        ball fan, the statistician—

Readers question what is not understood about this list. It seems
easy enough to visualize with the vivid, active verbs. For the
animals, and perhaps even the critic, the actions are instinctive.
Does that by extension mean that these actions are genuine? For
Moore, the answer would appear to be no, and that suggests that
for art to happen, there needs to be more than simply the
instinctive and the raw, there needs to be a means of ordering it,
a greater truth that binds the raw to the genuine. The instinctive
is ultimately not enough to satisfy the demands of art. She
extends the thought defending "'business documents and school-
books'" from Tolstoy's dismissive comments in his diary, "Where
the boundary between prose and poetry lies, I shall never be able
to understand. The question is raised in manuals of style, yet the
answer to it lies beyond me. Poetry is verse: prose is not verse.
Or else poetry is everything with the exception of business
documents and school books." Moore provides his commentary
in the notes to the poem, suggesting that she not only wants to
give credit where it is due, but also that she wants to not be
derivative to the point of incomprehension. Instead, she
broadens Tolstoy's discussion, arguing again that poetry being
called such is dependent upon the savvy and artistry of the artist
and his/her ordering principles, not necessarily the subject. She
acknowledges the relative import of all things made by man;
however, Moore enjoys her distinctions and classifications, the
intricacy of the argument and its refinement fuels the poem.

    She claims:
                            ...One must make a distinction
        however: when dragged into prominence by half poets, the result is not
        poetry,

nor till the poets among us can be
"literalists of
the imagination"—above
insolence and triviality and can present

for inspection, "imaginary gardens with real toads in them," shall we have
it.

Here, Moore borrows a phrase from Yeats's critique of Blake who argued, "The limitation of his view was from the very intensity of his vision; he was a too literal realist of imagination, as others are of nature; and because he believed that the figures seen by the mind's eye, when exalted by inspiration, were 'eternal existences,' symbols of divine essences, he hated every grace of style that might obscure their lineaments." Yeats argues against clarity at the expense of grace; Moore defers to both the raw and the genuine as paramount as opposed to the fiddle of the stylistic. Still, it is hard to believe that a poet so obsessed with syllabics would truly believe in a poetry without some form of style, whether it be metrical, rhythmic, or linguistic. Moore answers this point in keeping the poem in free verse, as if to assert the validity of her claim against "fiddle." The imaginary gardens can only be created, not by stylistic cartwheels, but by the ugly, visceral toad, a creature known to all and understood from its long context of fairy tales and warts. The toad seems inextricably tied to the real; populate the garden with enough toads, metaphorically speaking, and the garden will become an imagined experience for the reader, eliciting the active response of the first stanza, a response that Moore is careful to suggest *can* happen, if given the proper stimuli.

As she finishes the poem, so too Moore finishes the if/then construction with which she began.

...In the meantime, if you demand on the one hand,
the raw material of poetry in
all its rawness and
that which is on the other hand
genuine, you are interested in poetry.

Moore completes her aesthetic statement. Readers looking for the careful description, the image in all its relative disarray and wartiness, should want it coupled with the higher motive of the genuine, some truth that makes the telling matter. Moore completes her lesson in rhetoric with a summation of her case, and a final inclusive appeal to her reader.

"Poetry"

R.P. BLACKMUR ON IMAGINATION AND LITERALISM

[R.P. Blackmur was one of the most influential critics of 20th century American poetry who published several books of criticism, including *The Double Agent: Essays in Craft and Elucidation*, *The Expense of Greatness*, *Language as Gesture: Essays in Poetry*, *The Lion and the Honeycomb: Essays in Solicitude and Critique*, among them. He also taught at Princeton and published a critical biography of Henry Adams. Here, he engages the ideas of literalism and the imagination in response to the Yeats quote and Moore's use of it.]

Miss Moore's poem says, centrally, that we cannot have poetry until poets can be "literalists of the imagination." The phrase is made from one in W. B. Yeats's essay, "William Blake and the Imagination." The cogent passage in Yeats reads: "The limitation of his [Blake's] view was from the very intensity of his vision; he was a too literal realist of the imagination, as others are of nature; and because he believed that the figures seen by the mind's eye, when exalted by inspiration, were 'eternal essences,' symbols or divine essences, he hated every grace of style that might obscure their lineaments." Yeats first printed his essay in 1897; had he written it when he wrote his postscript, in 1924, when he, too, had come to hate the graces which obscure, he would, I think; have adopted Miss Moore's shorter and wholly eulogistic phrase and called Blake simply a "literalist of the imagination,"[6] and found some other words to explain Blake's excessively arbitrary symbols. At any rate, in Miss Moore's version, the phrase has a bearing on the poem's only other overt reference, which is to Tolstoy's exclusion of "business documents and school books" from the field of poetry. Here her phrase leads to a profound and infinitely spreading distinction. Poets who can present, as she says they must, "imaginary gardens with real toads in them," ought also to be able to present, and indeed will if their interest lies that way, real school books and documents. The whole flux of experience and interpretation is appropriate subject matter to an imagination literal enough to see the poetry in it; an imagination, that is, as intent on the dramatic texture (on what is involved, is tacit, is immanent) of the quotidian, as the imagination of the painter is intent, in Velasquez, on the visual texture of lace. One is reminded here, too, of T. S. Eliot's dogma in reverse: "The spirit killeth; the letter giveth life"; and as with Eliot the result of his new trope is to refresh the original form by removing from it the dead part of its convention, so Miss Moore's object is to exalt the imagination at the expense of its conventional appearances: Her gardens are imaginary, which makes possible the reality of her toads. Your commonplace mind would have put the matter the other way round—with the good intention of the same thing—and would have achieved nothing but the sterile assertion of the imagination as a portmanteau of stereotypes: which is the most part of what we are used to see carried, by all sorts of porters, as poetic baggage.

It is against them, the porters and their baggage, that Miss Moore rails when she begins her poem on poetry with the remark: "I, too, dislike it: there are things that are important beyond all this fiddle." But in the fiddle, she discovers, there is a place for the genuine. Among the conventions of expression there is the possibility of vivid, particularized instances:

Hands that can grasp, eyes
that can dilate, hair that can rise
    if it must,

and so on. Such hands, hair, and eyes are, we well know, props and crises of poetastry, and are commonly given in unusable, abstract form, mere derivative gestures we can no longer feel; as indeed their actual experience may also be. They remain, however, exemplars of the raw material of poetry. If you take them literally and make them genuine in the garden of imagination, then, as the poem says, "you are interested in poetry." You have seen them in ecstasy, which is only to say beside themselves, torn from their demeaning context; and if you are able to give them a new form or to refresh them with an old form—whichever is more expedient—then you will have accomplished a poem.

Perhaps I stretch Miss Moore's intentions a little beyond the pale; but the process of her poem itself I do not think I have stretched at all—have merely, rather, presented one of the many possible descriptions by analogue of the poetic process she actually employs. The process, like any process of deliberate ecstasy, involves for the reader as well as the writer the whole complex of wakened sensibility, which, once awakened, must be both constrained and driven along, directed and freed, fed and tantalized, sustained by reason to the very point of seeing, in every rational datum—I quote from another poem, "Black Earth"—the "beautiful element of unreason under it." The quotidian, having been shown as genuine, must be shown no less as containing the strange, as saying more than appears, and, even more, as containing the print of much that cannot be said at all. Thus we find Miss Moore constantly presenting images the most explicit but of a kind containing inexhaustibly the inexplicable—whether in gesture or sentiment. She gives what we know and do not know; she gives in this poem, for example, "elephants pushing, a wild horse taking a roll, a tireless wolf under a tree," and also "the baseball fan, the statistician." We can say that such apposites are full of reminding, or that they make her poem husky with unexhausted detail, and we are on safe ground; but we have not said the important thing, we have not named the way in which we are illuminated, nor shown any sign at all that we are aware of the major operation performed—in this poem (elsewhere by other agents)—by such appositions. They are as they succeed the springboards—as when they fail they are the obliterating quicksands of ecstasy. In their variety and their contrasts they force upon us two associated notions; first we are led to see the elephant, the horse, the wolf, the baseball fan, and the statistician, as a group or as two groups detached by their given idiosyncrasies from their practical contexts, we see them beside themselves, for themselves alone, like the lace in Velasquez or the water-lights in Monet; and secondly, I think, we come to be aware, whether consciously or not, that these animals and these men are themselves, in their special activities, obsessed, freed, and beside themselves. There is an exciting quality which the pushing elephant and the baseball fan have in common; and our excitement comes in feeling that quality, so integral to the apprehension of life, as it were beside and for itself, not in the elephant and the fan, but in terms of the apposition in the poem.

Such matters are not credibly argued and excess of statement perhaps only confuses import and exaggerates value. As it happens, which is why this poem is chosen rather than another, the reader can measure for himself exactly how valuable this quality is; he can read the "same" poem with the quality dominant and again with the quality hardly in evidence. On page 31 in *Observations* the poem appears in thirteen lines; in *Selected Poems* it has either twenty-nine or thirty, depending on how you count the third stanza. For myself, there is the difference between the poem and no poem at all, since the later version delivers—where the earlier only announces—the letter of imagination. But we may present the differences more concretely, by remarking that in the earlier poem half the ornament and all the point are lacking. What is now clearly the dominant emphasis on poets as literalists of the imagination— which here germinates the poem and gives it career, is not even implied in the earlier version. The poem did not get that far, did not, indeed, become a poem at all. What is now a serious poem on the nature of esthetic reality remained then a half-shrewd, half-pointless conceit against the willfully obscure. But it is not, I think, this rise in level from the innocuous to the penetrating, due to any gain in the strength of Miss Moore's conception. The conception, the idea, now that we know what it is, may be as readily inferred in the earlier version as it is inescapably felt in the later, but it had not in the earlier version been articulated and composed, had no posture to speak of, had lacked both development and material to develop: an immature product. The imaginary garden was there but there were no real toads in it.

NOTES

6. My quotation is taken from the collected edition of Yeats's essays, New York, 1924, page 147; Miss Moore's reference, which I have not checked, was to the original *Ideas of Good and Evil*, printed some twenty years earlier by A. H. Bullen.

—R.P. Blackmur. "The Method of Marianne Moore." *Marianne Moore: A Collection of Critical Essays.* Ed. Charles Tomlinson (Englewood Cliffs: Prentice Hall, 1969): 71–74.

BONNIE COSTELLO ON 'IMAGINARY GARDENS WITH REAL TOADS IN THEM'

[Bonnie Costello is a Professor of English at Boston University. She has written several books of criticism, *Elizabeth Bishop: Questions of Mastery, Wallace Stevens: The Poetics of Modernism,* and *Marianne Moore: Imaginary Possessions.* In this essay, Costello expounds on the historical value of the toad and the way in which it interacts with the notions of the raw and the genuine.]

The "literalist of the imagination," we infer, not only is "sincere" in his vision "untempted by any grace of style that might obscure its lineaments"), but also is successful in rendering that vision supremely graceful. In him, the formal and the natural are copresent, even cooperative; he produces "imaginary gardens with real toads in them." What follows is a contradictory demand for "the raw material of poetry," language and its various ordering devices (surprisingly aligned with the garden), and the genuine, things as they are (aligned with real toads). We lack the means to bring them into the same ontological status.

> In the meantime, if you demand on the one hand,
> the raw material of poetry in
>   all its rawness and
>   that which is on the other hand
>   genuine, you are interested in poetry.

Clear enough. But why toads? Why not "real roses" or "real princes"? Why must the oxymoron be double? A practical answer is that Moore feels an affinity for odd creatures. Indeed, her poems are full of them: her octopus, pangolin, jerboa, lizard, all "supreme in their abnormality," work against the curve of the general, the average. They are original and individual. The peculiar is linked in her mind with the particular. By their peculiarity they demonstrate the inclusiveness of the genuine, which will not discriminate against toads any more than against "business documents and school-books." The "poetic" ideally is a totally inclusive class. Moore "dislikes" poetry that statically congratulates itself on remaining within a class of what is "properly poetic." The wakeful mind is challenged to extend the class it can embrace. The genuine pressures decorum. Still, though the ideal objective viewer has no predilection for beauty but responds genuinely, we in fact do find toads "and the like" disconcerting, or if we do not, we know we are unusual in this. The norm of response to toads is, in life, not garden ease but hands that grasp, eyes that dilate, hair that rises, responses that also accompany the sublime.

Toads belong to a lexicon of symbols and have their own literary history, as rich as the history of the imaginary garden, even part of the same tradition. Together with other amphibians and reptiles (snakes, basilisks, chameleons) they often represent the power of the irrational in the midst of controlled elements. Their shocking, irregular appearance, their way of leaping out of camouflage, produces an effect of the uncanny, or gothic horror, in some versions of the sublime. Though "natural symbols," they are often cousins to the demonic or supernatural—the incubus, the satyr—as creatures outside the realm of human understanding. They are present in literature not as "things in themselves" but as challenges to the boundaries of beauty, decorum, human order.

We have not learned the method of Moore's "literalists of the imagination" who are at ease with toads. We have only their raw materials and their intentions. Indeed, their accomplishment seems to us miraculous, a matter of enchantment or alchemy— such as would turn princes into toads, and vice versa. It is hard to resist the conjecture that such suggestions of magical transformation were present in Moore's mind in a poem about poetry, about image-making. To the "literalists of the imagination" the toad is a prince again, welcome back into the decorum of the garden. Similarly, things and words, nature and spirit are for them all of the same order of being. But such an ideal belongs to an imaginary, Edenic garden. We, on earth, can create "conjuries that endure" (*Predilections*, 32), but they remain fictions. Our toads are conspicuous and vulgar, challenging the perimeters of formal beauty. It is the incongruity that stimulates us, not the perspective it ideally provides. In this realm of pseudomagic, of conjuring, what has happened to the genuine, which had been implying the mundane world, "things in themselves," "dry, hard, finite objects"? Freud suggests that the effect of the uncanny (*heimlich*) involved the strangeness of the familiar, as its etymology (both homely and strange) implies. Perhaps this same doubleness obtains in Moore's use of the genuine. As ordinary as toads are, we cannot find forms that can domesticate them. Indeed it is the very effort to frame them that makes them seem extraordinary.

Until the toad is a prince, the ideal "garden" is only imaginary. The toad is, in a sense, the emblem of failure, the rough edge of our attempt to bring the real world and the world of formal beauty together. It is also, because it confounds, an object of admiration (making our eyes "dilate"). That which is beyond language produces the effect of gusto, cousin to the sublime. But the toad is not an emblem of defeat. The point is not that we want to capture the toad in all his naturalness, the physical object itself as toad. Why should we? We have it aplenty in the world as it is. But "lit with piercing glances" (whether of reflected or radiated light Moore doesn't specify) the poeticized toad has the occasional look of a prince. It is "hair-raising" when you think about it, how we catch these transformations in transit but cannot complete the charm. We make mutations, gargoyles. We do read poetry, do become for moments "literalists of the imagination," but we cannot sustain our transformation. Sincerity, which started out as honest vision, becomes an expression of desire (not attainment), and the energy that accompanies that desire is "gusto." Moore's poems are "conjuries" that can make "real toads" appear in fictive gardens. But she always reveals what's up her sleeve, brings her images round to reveal the conjurer. She quotes, with approval, a saying of Kenneth Burke's: "The hypnotist has a way out *and* a way in" (*Predilections*, 8). Working against the beliefs of the literalist of the imagination, for whom poetry is presence, is the skeptic, for whom it is mere illusory "fiddle."

—Bonnie Costello. *Imaginary Possessions* (Cambridge: Harvard University Press, 1981): 22–24.

John M. Slatin on Moore's Place between Modernism and a Conservative Aesthetic

[John M. Slatin teaches at the University of Texas. He is the author of *Savage's Romance*, a critical exploration of Marianne Moore's poetry. Here, he tries to place Moore in a historical and aesthetic context somewhere between modernism and a more conservative sensibility.]

By the summer of 1919, when "Poetry" appears in *Others*, the isolated position Moore had begun to define for herself as she sought to escape the fate of Turgenev's Superfluous Man has become a position of some authority as well. It is a strange authority, though, because it does not depend on Moore's having sided with Pound, Eliot, and other exponents of the "new" in their struggle against the "established conventions of poetry." On the contrary, Moore's authority depends precisely on her continuing refusal to take sides, on her ability to transform her sense of isolation into something closely analogous to Hawthorne's "neutral territory"—a ground, that is, where the radical poetics of modernism, of *The Egoist* and *Others*, may meet and fuse with the conservative aesthetic espoused by *The Literary Digest* and by the poet's mother. In Moore's work generally, and in "Poetry" in particular, apparently irreconcilable positions are brought into combination, with the result that each position "imbues itself with the nature of the other," as Hawthorne says "the Actual and the Imaginary may" do under the right conditions[58]—though, like "real toads" in "imaginary gardens," each retains its own integrity as well. At the same time, both positions—in this case the modernist and the reactionary—are endowed with Moore's own neutrality and are thereby removed from the "category" of poetry.

By 1919, Moore has come to judge herself very much as critics like Louis Untermeyer and Harriet Monroe would judge her two years later.[59] She does not consider herself to be writing as a poet. She sees herself rather as an "interested" observer, one who is separated from poetry as by the "locked doors" of "Sojourn in the Whale" and looking through a partially opaque lens at her own work and that of her contemporaries—and what she sees does not strike her as meriting her title. For she sees a group of "autocrats"—herself among them—busily passing judgment and prescribing aesthetic criteria like Oliver Wendell Holmes at the Breakfast-Table, a disunited collection of "Critics and Connoisseurs" who have so far proved incapable of rising "above / insolence and triviality" to deliver "the genuine" article called "Poetry."[60]

We may say, then, that the isolation Moore enjoys in "Poetry" and from which she derives her authority is very different from the isolation she had feared so much in "So far as the future is concerned." She begins by claiming to "dislike" poetry—a strange admission from one who seems to be presenting herself as a poet. But even as this confession isolates her from us, it draws us by rhetorical means into a stance very much like hers. "I too, dislike it," she confides: evidently there is a community of people who share Moore's distaste for poetry, and evidently Moore considers that we, "too," are among its citizens. That community, moreover, is larger than we might think.

In an essay called "Impressionism," published in *Poetry* in September 1913, Ford Madox Hueffer writes that his own youthful "attempt to read Tennyson, Swinburne and Browning and Pope" had given rise to "a settled dislike for poetry" from which he had never fully recovered.[61] He justifies that "dislike" on the grounds that his reading had left him with the distinct impression that "all poets must of necessity write affectedly, at great length, with many superfluous words"—defects Hueffer spent the rest of his career trying to eliminate not only from his own work but also, crucially, from Pound's.[62] The "perfect contempt" with which Hueffer rejects "Tennyson, Swinburne and Browning and Pope" in a single breath seems consciously hyperbolic, just as Moore's does; but it is necessary. For if we dismiss his comments as absurd or unfair, we will be confounded by the words of the young George Santayana, explaining (in an essay republished just two years earlier) that "When Ossian, mentioning the sun, says it is round as the shield of his father, the expression is poetical. Why? Because he has added to the word sun, in itself sufficient and unequivocal, other words, unnecessary to practical clearness...."[63]

The philosopher may be right about Ossian; but Hueffer and Pound and Moore would say that he is exactly wrong in his account of what makes an expression "poetical." It is easy to imagine Hueffer responding to this pronouncement as he responded to Pound's *Canzoni* in 1911—by throwing himself on the floor and rolling with laughter;[64] but we do not have to guess at Pound's answer, or Moore's. Pound's response, learned the hard way from Hueffer, is the second rule of Imagisme: the injunction "To use absolutely no word that does not contribute to the presentation." Moore's is in "To a Snail": "'compression is the first grace of style.'"[65]

Moore responds in a more complex way in "Poetry." Having implied her allegiance to Hueffer and Pound, Moore separates herself from them by insisting that "there are things that are important beyond all this fiddle" and suggesting a means by which those "things" may be discovered: "Reading it, however, with a perfect contempt for it, one discovers that there is in / it after all, a place for the genuine." That "perfect contempt" is the necessary antidote to the poet's incessant "fiddle" with unnecessary words, and to the reader's fiddling as well.

We must not assume, however, that the phrase "perfect contempt" simply designates the feeling one has while reading poetry, or even what one ought to feel. It is not really a feeling, and it is not so much a by-product of reading as it is a way of reading—a means by which the reader may "stand outside and laugh," as "New York" suggests one must, in order to avoid getting "lost." A few other poems will help us to define the *virtú* of "perfect contempt" more clearly.

It is what Moore calls in "In This Age of Hard Trying Nonchalance Is Good And—" a "polished wedge" to drive between oneself and the poem one is reading, a "weapon" like that "self-protectiveness" which, as Moore writes in the same poem, is most clearly revealed by a "feigned inconsequence of manner." It is also one of "Those Various Scalpels" used in the laboratory to "dissect" specimens and in the operating theater to remove dead or diseased tissue and restore the body to health.[66] William Carlos Williams, writing in *The Dial* in 1925, offers a useful description of its practical value (though he is not talking specifically about "perfect contempt") when he writes:

> Miss Moore gets great pleasure from wiping soiled words or cutting them clean out, removing the aureoles that have been pasted about them or taking them bodily from greasy contexts.... With Miss Moore a word is a word most when it is separated out by science, treated with acid to remove the smudges, washed, dried and placed right side up on a clean surface. Now one may say that this is a word. Now it may be used....[67]

Like her writing, Moore's reading is guided by a certain edginess, an urge to penetrate quickly and get out fast, for protracted involvement is risky: "to go in is to be lost." But "perfect contempt" affords her exactly the narrow standpoint she needs— a position from which she may "discover" in what she reads "a place for the genuine" without having to "go in" herself.

NOTES

58. Nathaniel Hawthorne, "The Custom-House," *The Centenary Edition of the Works of Nathaniel Hawthorne* (Columbus, Ohio, 1962), 1:36.

59. Harriet Monroe, et al., "A Symposium on Marianne Moore," *Poetry* 19 (Jan. 1922): 208–16. See also Louis Untermeyer, *American Poetry Since 1900* (New York, 1923), 346ff.

60. "Critics and Connoisseurs," *Others* 3 (July 1916): 4.

61. Ford Madox Hueffer, "Impressionism—Some Speculations," Part II *Poetry* 2 (Sept. 1913): 217.

62. Ibid.

63. George Santayana, "The Elements and Function of Poetry," in *Interpretations of Poetry and Religion* (1900; rpt. New York, 1911), 261–62.

64. Kenner, *The Pound Era* (Berkeley and Los Angeles, 1971), 80.

65. *O*, 23.

66. "Those Various Scalpels," *Contact* 1 (Jan. 1921): 1–2; reprinted from the Bryn Mawr College *Lantern*, where it appeared in 1918.

67. Tomlinson, 57.

—John M. Slatin. *The Savage's Romance* (State College: The Pennsylvania State University Press, 1986): 40–43.

Bonnie Honigsblum on Moore's Revisions as Representative of Her Modernism

[Bonnie Honigsblum is the author of "Marianne Moore's Revisions of 'Poetry'" In this excerpt, Honigsblum treats Moore's multiple revisions as symptomatic of her modernism.]

Even prior to the revision of 1967, some had embraced the five-stanza version of "Poetry" as a modernist document. In *The Influence of Ezra Pound*, K. L. Goodwin, claiming that "her natural predilection for precise, objective description found convenient theoretical justification in Imagism, which she has practised assiduously throughout her career," declares that in "Poetry" Moore states that "poetry must be made up ... of what is 'genuine', of 'raw material ... in all its rawness'." Goodwin asserts that Moore distinguishes between a symbolic and an imagistic use of this material in the same way that Pound does in his article "Vorticism" (157–58). In the same vein, Jean Garrigue called "Poetry" one of the nine poems in which Moore is both "poet and critic, writing incidentally about literature in general or poetry in particular" (204). Not only is this a modernist subject, it is also a modernist treatment, in Garrigue's view establishing "a new touchstone," which "is not the old and famous *beautiful and true*" but the "genuine" which is, then, the "*useful*" (Garrigue qtd. in Unger 204). Garrigue concludes:

> Seemingly straightforward, it is oblique when you look into it and complex in terms of what's left out as well as what's put in. And with its iconoclastic and reformist frankness it is upsetting a good many applecarts.

What could be more modernist?

Moore herself supplied the answer when she revised "Poetry" once again in 1967 for the first edition of her *Complete Poems*. She cut the poem to all but its first three lines and put a new revision of the five-stanza version in a note, retaining the notes that had come to append the five-stanza version, which became notes on a note to the three-line version of 1967. In one stroke, she transformed the poem, in one sense revealing the skeleton that had been there since 1919. As a self-conscious modernist—stubbornly resisting postmodernism—she reverted to an Imagist technique, perhaps grown overly familiar by the 1960s, revealing the image-within-the-image, and she deployed a modernist device, appending footnotes, a method that both Pound and Eliot had explored. In this context, her drastic revisions of 1967 seem at worst playful and at best an insightful homage to a mellowing tradition, all too susceptible of parody. What saves the 1967 revision of "Poetry" in this respect is its conscious, even self-conscious, regard for its sources—that revision of the original, five-stanza version, imbedded in a footnote.

In an important sense, the three-line version of "Poetry" with its elaborate, perhaps even ridiculous note, is Moore's precursor to this variorum text of the poem. Besides confirming the relationships among various versions of "Poetry" suggested by Moore's revision of it for the 1967 printing of *Complete Poems*, this variorum text of "Poetry" highlights what might be called the spirit or core of the poem, whatever remained intact throughout the revisionary process. It establishes that certain parts of "Poetry" never changed (if we consider the notes to the 1967 revision part of the poem): the title and the final word, "poetry"; the opening disclaimer, "I too dislike it"; a miscellany of "phenomena"; the importance of the "genuine"; and the rhetorical device of a speaker addressing an audience, an "I" and a "you," in the case of the three-stanza version the "you" suggested only by the locution "I too" and later, "we know." These elements afford a central unit to which Moore added an assortment of related pieces. But this dressing and undressing of the mannequin, so to speak, was a conscious technique rather than the attention-seeking gesture some critics have made it out to be. On the contrary, the revisions of the poem as evidenced in the variorum text appended here prove a case for "Poetry" as Moore's personal expression of her views of modernism in poetry and her own modernist method.

—Bonnie Honigsblum. "Marianne Moore's Revisions of 'Poetry.'" *Marianne Moore: Woman and Poet*. Ed. Patricia C. Willis (Orono, ME: The National Poetry Foundation, University of Maine, 1990): 194–196.

JEFFREY D. PETERSON ON CHANGING THE 'PLACE' OF POETRY

[In this essay, Peterson discusses the way in which Moore broadens notions of where poetry can happen and what the criteria are.]

While it's true that the indices to both editions of *Observations* are unique in Moore's work, they may enable us to see something *in* the poem(s) "Poetry" frequently "missed by the externalist." I want to suggest, first, that the poem-as-notes, "Poetry" (1967), shares its textual self-consciousness with the indices-as-poems in both editions of *Observations*, and that these formal gestures of Moore's are analogously new in poeticizing different sorts of referential frames within *the book* as we know it. If we grant Moore's "Notes" the context of poetic "place" they request, then the presence of "Poetry" (*CMP* 266–68) in them establishes the work as a sort of poem-within-the-poem-of-notes as apparatus. We begin by asking: where do the excerpts from Tolstoy and Yeats in the 1951 text of "Poetry" stand in relation to other such texts in *Complete Poems*? Tentatively, we might venture that the excerpts seem somehow further "inside" (or "outside") the normative context of material established in Moore's "Notes" (*CMP* 261–98). That is, since they refer to a variorum before the note which refers to the poem "proper" (*CMP* 36) is complete, Tolstoy and Yeats seem to stand "further away" from the rest of "Notes" as textual frame. This complication tempted George Nitchie to refer to the texts from Yeats and Tolstoy here as "subfootnotes" (41). Whether or not such a relation can be meaningfully fixed in the volume, the anomalous presence of "Poetry" (1951) in Moore's "Notes" (1967) asks us to consider it. The real value of "subfootnotes," then, is that "Poetry" seems to elude it; that Nitchie's term records an attempt, however problematic, to trace the shifting textual frames of "Poetry" within *Complete Poems*.

A "footnote to an excerpt from itself"—or excerpt from a footnote to itself—"Poetry" manages to insist cyclically upon the location of its text as a perplexing play of poetic "place." This play among overlapping textual frames is a formal enactment of what Kenneth Burke calls the "secondary level" of theme in Moore's "Four Quartz Crystal Clocks" (Burke 89). Burke's thematic interest here is "not the theme of clocks that tell the time, but of clocks that tell the time to clocks that tell the time." He considers this "thoroughly symbolic, as signalizing a concern not merely for the withinness of motives, but for the withinness-of-withinness of motives, the motives behind motives" in Moore's poetics. There may be more to the final form of "Poetry"—a poem of indeterminate "withinness"—than the Schulman interview alone would lead us to believe.

—Jeffrey D. Peterson. "Notes on the Poem(s) 'Poetry': The Ingenuity of Moore's Poetics Place." *Marianne Moore: Woman and Poet*. Ed. Patricia C. Willis (Orono, ME: The National Poetry Foundation, University of Maine, 1990): 226–227.

JEANNE HEUVING ON THE CONFLICT BETWEEN MODES OF SEEING

[Jeanne Heuving is an Associate Professor of English at the University of Washington at Bothell. She has published *Omissions Are Not Accidents: Gender in the Art of Marianne Moore*. In this essay, Heuving reflects on the conflicts in modes of seeing.]

Most of Moore's poems published between 1918 and 1921 are either meditations on perspective and artistic vision or are direct seeings. Images, on the one hand, of light, transparency, and clarity, and on the other hand, of darkness, opacity, and deflection are prominent. Beginning frequently in desire for the former and the related values of "simplicity, harmony, and truth," these poems usually conclude by establishing the opposite and the values of particularity, complexity, and tentativeness. Although in her prose writings of this time Moore frequently upholds qualities of transcendence and universality, when these values are put to the test in her poetry, they are undermined. And while at this time Moore is turning away from syllabic verse toward free verse, seemingly in an effort to clarify and simplify her writing, her meanings do not reflect this same transparency.[16] Indeed, Moore is struggling to attain the Modernist edict of "direct treatment of the 'thing,'" but her own position in the culture as a woman leads her to write an indirect, complex poetry

In "Poetry" and "In the Days of Prismatic Colour," the conflict between mediated and unmediated seeing is addressed thematically Both poems postulate the prior existence of an original clarity or truth. "In the Days of Prismatic Colour" locates this time historically as coexisting with Adam: "Not in the days of Adam and Eve but when Adam / was alone." In "Poetry," this clarity and truth is expressed as "the genuine," which exists prior to and apart from its representation in poetry. Although both poems manifest a belief in, or perhaps merely a nostalgia for, an original and originating truth and clarity, neither purports to inscribe these qualities. In fact, both poems enlist opposing terms—"sophistication" and "complexity" in "in the Days of Prismatic Colour" and "the fiddle" of poetry in "Poetry"—and are caught up in the very qualities they initially seem to denounce. (...)

In "Poetry" Moore turns decisively away from the modes of contrariety and the fantastic, though the poem shares other characteristics of Moore's earlier adverse poetry Moving between address and description, she begins with her best known (adverse) line, "I, too, dislike it," and attempts, but fails, to provide a definition of poetry that is not "entangled in the negative." The terms and examples Moore uses to define poetry proliferate in a relation of supplementarity rather than unity, as can be seen in the displacement of "genuine" from the primary term to be investigated at the beginning of the poem to one of two terms—along with "raw material"—at the conclusion of the poem. Furthermore, Moore's implied audience changes from those who seem to have every right to dislike poetry to those who earn, through appropriate attention to poetry, the honorific comment: "then you are interested in poetry" The beginning and ending of the poem are as follows:

> I, too, dislike it: there are things that are important beyond all
>   this fiddle.
> Reading it, however, with a perfect contempt for it, one
>   discovers in
> it after all, a place for the genuine..
>
>   In the meantime, if you demand on the one hand,
> the raw material of poetry in
>   all its rawness and
>   that which is on the other hand
>   genuine, then you are interested in poetry

In "Poetry" Moore is caught between two conflicting impulses: the need and desire to define poetry universally and generally—to "come / At the cause of the shouts"—and to engage irreducible particulars and expressions.[22] While in her later collage poetry she allows whatever positive definition her poems provide to emerge in and through juxtaposed elements, here she is pulled in two directions at once, much like the bat in this poem, "holding on upside down or in quest of something to / eat." Notably, Moore does not attempt to define poetry from her position as maker but as audience—a position that enables her to establish her stance "elsewhere."

NOTES

16. Slatin links Moore's change from syllabic to free verse forms in 1921-25 to her shift away from what he describes as her "isolationist tendencies." However, he does not explain why in her later poetry, in which she is presumably even less of an "isolationist," she reverts to syllabics (see *Savage's Romance*, especially 3–4).

22. See Chapter 3, n. 41.

—Jeanne Heuving. *Omissions Are Not Accidents: Gender in the Art of Marianne Moore*. (Detroit: Wayne State University Press, 1992): 87–88, 90–91.

E.R. GREGORY ON DERIVATION

[E.R. Gregory is the author of *Milton and The Muses* and many scholarly articles. Here, the author expands on the notion of derivation in the poem.]

Up to a point Moore admits the use of older poets as an aid in writing the ideal poetry that is "original and lucid."[4] For her, the great divide between the acceptably and the excessively derivative is whether the poet truly adapts her source or merely copies it. Thus, she takes a criticism that Yeats had leveled at Blake, namely, that he was "too literal a realist of imagination" and reverses it, stating that we cannot have genuine poetry

till the poets among us can be
"literalists of

the imagination"—above
insolence and triviality....

Her challenge to Yeats exemplifies a use of the past that goes beyond mere repetition to create insight, a use that reflects the critical stance that she took in her prose. Commenting on Elizabeth Bishop's poetry, for example, she wrote that "we cannot ever be wholly original ... Our best and newest thoughts ... have been known to past ages." She added, however, a significant caveat: "an indebted thing does not interest us unless there is originality underneath it."[5] She gives no pat prescriptions as to how artists are to use the past without becoming unduly derivative. But her own practice seems the safest guide to what she meant, with "Poetry" itself, addressing a topic older than Horace, yet unmistakably twentieth-century in

language and spirit, as brilliant an example of the genuine and
the intelligible as we could wish.

Notes

4. Bonnie Costello, *Marianne Moore: Imaginary Possessions* (Cambridge,
Mass.: Harvard U P, 1981) 20.

5. *Complete Prose* (New York: Viking, 1986) 328.

—E. R. Gregory. "Moore's Poetry." *The Explicator* 52, no. 1 (Fall
1993): 45–46.

CRITICAL ANALYSIS OF

"Marriage"

In 1913, Picasso brought cubism to America in the New York Armory Show; Marianne Moore clipped six articles about the show and pasted them into her scrapbook. Though Picasso's famous collage innovations were not among those shown, certainly the notion of cubism and Moore's awareness of other collage-like modernist poems may easily have lead Moore into thinking about her own collage. In 1923, she wrote to her brother, claiming that she wanted "Marriage" to offend people. The poem first appeared as a chapbook by Monroe Wheeler's Maniken Press, in a limited press run of 200.

"Marriage" is one of Moore's longest and bravest works. She chose an unusual format, that of collage, which provided ample opportunity to marry the words of friends with the words of magazines, journals, and books. Moore changes perspective constantly, switching from Adam to Eve to disinterested narrator, and if we are to assume that the narrator is Moore herself, then the narrator places herself in a strange position as the authority on an enterprise into which she never entered. She commented that she believed marriage was perfect for everyone save herself. Still, as a writer and a moralist, she firmly believed herself able to judge the efforts of those around her: Warner and Constance, Bryher and McAlmon, and Alyse Gregory and Llewelyn Powys. With these people in mind, her poem almost necessarily offers variegated points of view.

The poem begins with an almost business-like comment, that is immediately qualified, as if the rhetoric were inappropriate for so public a proposition. She writes:

This institution,
perhaps one should say enterprise
out of respect for which
one says one need not change one's mind
about a thing one has believed in,
requiring public promises

of one's intention
to fulfill a private obligation:

Clearly, Moore disapproves of the public avowal of emotional commitments that would be better shared between two rather than requisite crowds and witnesses. The place of the crowd seems only to notarize the agreement rather than to offer any sort of added emotional depth to the vows. After this initial statement of exigence, Moore chooses to take as her prototypes for marriage, the first married couple of the Judeo-Christian religion. She wonders what Adam and Eve think of marriage now, after having lived it since humankind began. In her wondering, she invokes Francis Bacon, quoting, "'of circular traditions and impostures,/ committing many spoils,'/, requiring all one's criminal ingenuity/ to avoid." She uses Bacon to create a sort of secular ethos, wherein marriage is intellectualized into another facet in the study of rhetoric and business. While the circular tradition of marriage may well be the ring, it might also be the constant struggle for power or, coupled with the impostures, it may also be the rhetoric that brings people together, the audition of dating, the art of persuasion, the double speak required to win the hand of the partner. Ultimately, as Moore claims as per Bacon, the victor has the spoils of power and control. Throughout the poem Moore presents the vehicle of speech and the ability to articulate as central to commanding the other in the relationship.

She then claims that though we have psychology, which supposedly "explains everything," it still explains nothing about the human heart and the interaction between the sexes. She takes for example Eve. Eve presents as a beautiful woman with an astounding facility for language: she is "able to write simultaneously/ in three languages—/ English, German, and French—/ and talk in the meantime." Moore mentions in her notes that the germ of this multi-lingual model came from an article in *Scientific American*, "Multiple Consciousness or Reflex Action of Unaccustomed Range" wherein a woman can perform the same tasks as the mythical Eve. Left to her own devices, Eve is articulate in multiple languages and in control of each. Still, she contrarily wants both a "commotion" and "quiet." Eve claims "*I* should like to be alone;" unfortunately, Adam is not prepared for that to happen, he claims to have the same want of being solitary, and he suggests "why not be alone together?" Eve's contained self and world wherein she can articulate her desire is suddenly met with an intruder, who claims in his own "circular" rhetoric to want the same as she, and to be able to attain their mutual desires.

In the next lines, Moore leaps suddenly from the tête á tête between Eve and Adam to describe the beauty of Eden, where both the stars and the forbidden fruit appear "incandescent." There is temptation everywhere and "its existence is too much;/ it tears one to pieces/ and each fresh wave of consciousness/ is poison." The stage is set for the Fall of Man, and Eve finds herself distracted by the too-present Adam. In the next lines, Moore asks us to look again at Eve, "'See her, see her in this common world,'/ the central flaw/ in that first crystal-fine experiment." Moore figures Eve as the instigator of marriage as she is the first to make humankind aware of its nakedness, leading subsequently to the marriage bed, etc. Still, Moore suggests that the first incarnation of Adam and Eve in the garden was only "this amalgamation which can never be more/ than an interesting impossibility." Perhaps marriage was simply never meant to truly work, if even those wed in literal bliss could not stay the course, getting themselves in trouble their first time out. As Moore directs our attention to Eve, she can also be heard to refer to marriage as

> "that strange paradise
> unlike flesh, stones,
> gold or stately buildings,
> the choicest piece of my life:
> the heart rising
> in its estate of peace
> as a boat rises
> with the rising of the water"
> constrained in speaking of the serpent—
> shed snakeskin in the history of politeness

not to be returned again—
that invaluable accident
exonerating Adam.

The quote comes from Richard Baxter's *The Saints' Everlasting Rest* and refers to the saints in the final communion with God in heaven. Moore creates a heaven of sorts for Eve, wherein she gives over to the command and thrall of Adam and in so doing loses all of her ability to articulate. She has traded her language and understanding for his, as a wife is expected. She is not to speak of the attraction of the serpent or the lure of knowledge; indeed, she is to forget the snake except when she is recalling while Adam is in charge. It was Eve that ate the fruit and is therefore guilty, and Adam who sacrificed himself to help her. When Moore writes the lines, the sneer seems clear; it is more than good luck that the Bible story reinforces the patriarchy.

Then Moore switches her attention to Adam, describing him as beautiful and dangerous. She takes the words of Philip Littell who described George Santayana's poems in *New Republic*, writing, "We were puzzled and we were fascinated, as if by something feline, by something colubrine." The feeling is echoed by Moore in describing Adam as "a crouching mythological monster," a sexual predator. She then places Adam in a "Persian miniature" with a leopards and giraffes, predators and prey. At this point, Adam too is at the height of his powers of speech:

Alive with words,
vibrating like a cymbal
touched before it has been struck,
he has prophesied correctly—
"the speedy stream
which violently hears all before it,
at one time silent as the air
and now as powerful as the wind."
"Treading chasms
on the uncertain footing of a spear."

Moore takes the words from Hazlitt's "Essay on Burke's Style" to figure her character. Adam is alive with the possibilities of what he might be able to achieve. With speech only for himself, he has already navigated with ease the act of prophesy and presumably that of naming. He is now ready to move on to an audience. He sets his sights on Eve, "forgetting that there is in woman/ a quality of mind/ which as an instinctive manifestation/ is unsafe." Eve is indeed unsafe with her verbal acuity and Adam's easily won pride. He speaks to her in the words of Richard Baxter, an American Puritanical writer, pontificating on "past states, the present state,/ seals, promises,/ the evil one suffered,/ the good one enjoys/ hell, heaven,/ everything convenient/ to promote one's joy." The words are formal, indicating both Adam's strain and his verbal unease in speaking to Eve. Still, Eve is enchanted by his speech and Adam "experiences a solemn joy/ in seeing that he has become an idol." This time Moore cuts words from Anatole France in creating Adam.

By the next lines, Moore has jumped again to a new idea. She starts with a nightingale that plagues Adam. One is immediately reminded of the story of Tereus and Procne, a married couple of Greek myth. Procne sends Tereus, her husband, to fetch her sister, Philomela for her. Tereus does get her sister, and en route home, rapes her and then cuts her tongue out so that she might not tell her sister of his crime. Philomela foils him by weaving his assault into a tapestry. The gods have pity on their mutual suffering and turn all into birds. Pointedly for this story, the wounded wife becomes a nightingale. With the mythic association, one can only imagine what transgressions Moore imagined of Adam as he listens to the nightingale/wife and "its silences." Moore combines the myth with a quote from Edward Thomas's *Feminine Influence on the Poets*. She might have been referencing *The King's Quair* by James I, King of Scotland, where he sees the vision of a maiden outside his prison window and laments that he can neither go to her, nor bring her attention to him lest he scare her off. He is trapped into no response. He is "Unnerved by the nightingale/ and dazzled by the apple,/ "impelled by "the illusion of a fire/ effectual to extinguish fire,"/

compared with which/ the shining of the earth/ is but a deformity." Adam finds himself unsettled with the prophecy of the nightingale and enchanted with the forbidden fruit of this woman, Eve, of whom he knows little. His lust is merely the illusion of the fire that is love, a strong enough illusion perhaps to undermine any true fire. It is the difference between the easy earthbound love of body which can be destroyed versus that of the soul, which cannot be destroyed. Moore is taking people to task for their light-hearted entry into the state of marriage.

As for Adam himself, he finds marriage, in the words of William Godwin, husband of Mary Wollstonecraft, herself the author of *Vindication on the Rights of Woman*, to be "a very trivial object indeed," particularly because it seems to have upset Adam from his daily tasks. Indeed, the state of marriage is such a hindrance that Adam accuses Hymen, the god of marriage of being "unhelpful," a mere rhetorical end (as the hymen itself became) for love. Adam builds around the notion the ornamentation of flowers, and returns to this construct the sweet talking serpent, "the potent apple," all in the huge mouth of a hippopotamus. He continues claiming in the words of Anthony Trollope, from *Barchester Towers*, "that 'for love that will/ gaze an eagle blind,/ that is with Hercules/ climbing the trees/ in the garden of the Hesperides,/ from forty-five to seventy/ is the best age.'" Perhaps the best age because man can no longer act as the sexual predator of the earlier lines? He then makes his comment on marriage, "commending it as fine art, as an experiment, a duty or as merely recreation." His view accepts marriage as a largely social construct, a mode by which one might fulfill all of his appositives in a public way. Otherwise, who is to categorize the transaction between a man and a woman as duty or art? He claims that there must be "friction" and "the fight to be affectionate" making the whole 'enterprise' a kind of trial by fire experience. Nowhere is there mention of any sort of emotional bond. Men and women are still strangers of a sort, partners in a publicly owned business.

Moore then returns to the woman, likening her to a stalking panther, the hunting Diana, who is notably chaste. Moore takes from Ecclesiasticus a description of the huntress, "'darkeneth her countenance/ as a bear doth,'/ the spiked hand/ that has an affection for one/ and proves it to the bone,/ impatient to assure you/ that impatience is the mark of independence,/ not of bondage." Here she assures the man that her desire to be married to him is really about marriage as a freeing state for both man and woman. Moore takes this opportunity to inject the cynicism of C. Bertram Hartmann who claims:

"Married people often look that way"—
"seldom and cold, up and down,
mixed and malarial
with a good day and a bad."

Here, Moore incorporates a bit of conversation she preserved in her journals; the word play and images please her and help in modernizing the notion of marriage. She returns to the idea of the duplicity used to ensnare a partner as she talks about "We Occidentals" having lost ourselves and forgotten the irony of Esther's banquets ("the Ahasuerus tete a tete banquet") wherein she set Haman up for destruction. Moore illustrates the banquet table with "small orchids like snakes' tongues," returning to the serpent's knowledge, the danger of speech, and the idea of bondage with her reference to *The Tempest*. She begins to characterize the life of the modern married woman with the words of Comtesse de Noailles:

"four o'clock does not exist,
but at five o'clock
the ladies in their imperious humility
are ready to receive you":

Moore adds her own comment on the scene:

in which experience attests
that men have power
and sometimes one is made to feel it.

The women are using their own form of nonverbal rhetoric,

using their 'imperious humility' to handle men, recognizing it as a counterpoint in battle against men's use of patriarchal power to control the woman. In the social scene between the sexes, there is a constant vying for power. For men, power lies in having an attractive woman as wife, as can be seen in Moore's use of a quote from Mary Francis Nearing's parody, "The Rape of the Lock." The man's point of view continues when he speaks using a quote from A. Mitram Rihbany's *The Syrian Christ* where the author expounds on the value of a silent wife in 'the Orient.' He also claims, according to Moore's note, that "not all the angels in heaven could subdue a woman." Moore clearly satirizes his claim when she offers the words using a quote from the President Emeritus of Bryn Mawr College, M. Carey Thomas, who mentioned in the Founder's Address that "Men practically reserve for themselves stately funerals, splendid monuments, memorial statues, membership in academies, medals, titles, honorary degrees, stars, garters, ribbons, buttons and other shining baubles, so valueless in themselves and yet so infinitely desireable because they are symbols of recognition by their fellow craftsmen of difficult work well done." Moore splices the quote and begins with "Men are monopolists," again figuring men in business terms and suggesting the inequity between the sexes, claiming that individuals so obsessed with public symbols of 'success' are "unfit to be the guardians/ of another person's happiness."

The man retorts, referring to woman as 'mummies' who "must be handled carefully—/ 'the crumbs from a lion's meal,/ a couple of shins and the bit of an ear';/" The woman is an embalmed figure, already dead, the leftovers presumably of a sexual conquest, or another form of consumption of identity via the male predator. The degradation continues as Moore borrows words from Ezra Pound, who claimed " 'a wife is a coffin,'/ that severe object/ with the pleasing geometry/ stipulating space not people,/ refusing to be buried/ and uniquely disappointing,/ revengefully wrought in the attitude/ of an adoring child/ to a distinguished parent." Within nine lines, the woman is not a person, but an attractive receptacle, a coffin that won't be buried and a disappointment in that she becomes child-like in the presence of her controlling husband. Moore in an attempt to balance the damning comments of prototypical man offers the words of woman: she too is displeased with her mate, who, like a butterfly has "'proposed/ to settle on my hand for life'—/What can one do with it?" Clearly the reference to settling on her hand references not only the man, but his public symbol of the ring, a rhetorical move securing his territory. The woman asks not only what can be done with the man, but what else with this ring, valued perhaps as other baubles as a 'difficult work well done.' Sadly, as the poem continues the pair drift farther and farther away, each incapable of loving someone beyond him/herself.

The poem finally breaks away from the tedious bickering of the unhappy couple and returns to the observant narrator and her dismay and even disgust:

> What can one do for them—
> these savages
> condemned to disaffect
> all those who are not visionaries
> alert to undertake the silly task
> of making people noble?

Moore's commentary suggests that the only person foolish enough to try to link two fools is a politician, intent on the institution of marriage as a mode of making people seem better than they are. The model set forth also allows for people to leave each other due to overexposure; Moore steals the phrase from an advertisement in *English Review* that enumerates the reasons a woman might go shopping. When even advertisements offer commentary on matrimony, the public is too much with us. As one is leaving the marriage, the other prostrates, "'I am yours to command.'" And always, there is the public voice adding to the private domain of the union: "'Everything to do with love is mystery'" as per F.C. Tilney's translation of *The Original Fables of La Fontaine*. Moore adds that the mysteries of men and women and union cannot be solved in a day, or it seems human time as the prototypes for man and woman are the mismatched Adam and Eve. At the end of the assorted comments, Moore claims:

One sees that it is rare—
that striking grasp of opposites
opposed each to the other, not to unity,
which is cycloid inclusiveness
has dwarfed the demonstration
of Columbus with the egg—

Couples that long to be married in the social sense and not the
spiritual sense far outnumber those who would sacrifice part of
the individual to balance the whole. She references the story of
Christopher Columbus who, when asked to make an egg stand
on its end, chose to break the shell to do so. She uses the story to
illustrate the necessity of sacrifice if the marriage is to succeed.
She also reinforces the idea when she invokes 'that charitive
Euroclydon' the wind that, in Acts 27 destroyed Paul's boat, but
saved the lives of he and his men, reinforcing Moore's idea that
the wind can be fortuitous as well as devastating. Still, it remains
frightening because of it operates outside the realm of man's
control. As she watches the randomness of the love both found
and lost, she writes that she, for one, would be troubled at the
loss of love, that she, unlike the others, would not recover so
quickly from the loss of it.

She then enters into her final comments on the state of
marriage:

   …"I have encountered it
   among those unpretentious
   proteges of wisdom,
   where seeming to parade
   as the debater and the Roman,
   the statesmanship
   of an archaic Daniel Webster
   persists to their simplicity of temper
   as the essence of the matter:

   'Liberty and union
   now and forever',

the Book on the writing table;
the hand in the breast pocket."

Moore lets the last word fall to the publicists of love, the politicians who espouse the state. They claim that true freedom might be found in marriage, and the Bible on the table supports them, as the hand in the pocket bespeaks both their kept heart and their position of authority.

Ultimately, Moore chooses the collage because it is the most public of forms, creating the cacophony of commentary one hears about marriage, its form ranging from the self-absorbed modern man, to the petty bickering of Adam and Eve, to the Biblical commentary. Notably, in a poem filled with thirty quotations, only three of those were from women. Moore places herself not only in the Modernist tradition of the poem-collage, but also as one of the few female voices commenting on the state of marital bliss. Readers will duly note that the poem does not end with the comments of the entrenched couple; it ends instead on the words of the public official who links it inexorably to government and the status quo.

"Marriage"

PAMELA WHITE HADAS ON SOLITUDE AND THE SELF

[Pamela White Hadas has written four books of poetry and a book of criticism entitled *Marianne Moore: Poet of Affection*. In this excerpt, she discusses Moore's insistence on solitude as a necessary state for the poetic mind.]

"Marriage" is obscure for these reasons, for the brevity of its insights and the lack of smooth transitions between them. The poem is true to the "conscientious inconsistency" of the mind described by Moore in "The Mind Is an Enchanting Thing"; it is a poem that describes the poet's mind with as much faithfulness as it describes what is in the poet's mind. "Marriage" is constantly changing tones, seemingly in response to itself, its own inner need to leave an unsatisfactory phrase or unexplainable or unenlargeable image. Clearly Moore thinks of "marriage" not so much as an event as a set of attitudes toward a hypothesis. It is centrally concerned with mental, not physical actions, and it leads eventually to a marriage within one mind of its various attitudes toward marriage rather than to a marriage of different minds.

Moore's initial picture of Eve, for instance, marries the old mythy attractiveness with a very peculiar mental ability:

> Eve: beautiful woman—
> I have seen her
> when she was so handsome
> she gave me a start,
> able to write simultaneously
> in three languages—
> English, German, and French—
> and talk in the meantime;

This Eve gives us a start, too, but not because of her alleged handsomeness. Moore's note on this passage refers us to an article in the *Scientific American* entitled "Multiple Consciousness or Reflex Action of Unaccustomed Range." We are done with Eden. Babel is behind us. *Finnegans Wake* is before us, unwritten as yet, a threatening potential of multiple consciousness turned literary. Eve is modern and it is her mind, the incomprehensible comprehendability of it, that attracts us. But if amazing Eve is busy scribbling and talking at the same time, relying on unconscious fastidiousness, we suspect, as she could not possibly be *thinking* of everything "equally positive in demanding a commotion / and stipulating quiet," where is there room for dense old Adam? He enters the room of the poem and of the scribbling Eve when we are not looking; he is an unwelcome "visitor." "I should like to be alone," says preoccupied Eve,

> to which the visitor replies
> "I should like to be alone;
> why not be alone together?"

A modest proposition, surely. On the surface it is good natured enough, or pleasantly devious. Any second thought about it, though, is sure to be made uncomfortable with its glibness, vulgarity, and sad presumption with regard to what could be a sacred human relation. There is an insidious remoteness and literally embarrassing sentiment in the proposal of being alone together. It is all mildly funny, too, but the poem, resisting its own impulses with a vengeance, glances suddenly back to Eden and seriousness, as it was seen to glance for just a moment near the beginning, at a live goldenness. Here, despite a warning given earlier that "psychology ... explains nothing," we are offered a psychological reason:

> Below the incandescent stars
> below the incandescent fruit,
> the strange experience of beauty;
> its existence is too much;
> it tears one to pieces
> and each fresh wave of consciousness
> is poison.

We welcome the new inspiration and relief from the offhand proposition that immediately precedes it, but are we to welcome the news that each such fresh wave is poison? Although sudden beauty saves us from the poetic sterility of "alone together," it transports us to the only slightly more poetically fertile ground of being alone *alone*, savoring a disjunction of senses that we know is poison.

From affectation to affection, in poem after poem, Marianne Moore writes, or seems to write, in self-defense against this poison. At the same time she cannot help seeking it out. She may remind one of the small animal, observed observing, in her poem "An Octopus,"

> the victim on some slight observatory,
> of "a struggle between curiosity and caution,"
> inquiring what has scared it.

This is a "victim" not only of some hidden predatory thing in man or in nature, but of its own struggle between the instinctive desire to *know* and the fear that by venturing out to know, it will *be known*. In the poem "Marriage," no matter how much the mind wants to be alone, there is the very existence of "Adam" to contend with. Adam is tantamount to a world; he is the general "other" as well as the particular "other" who is dangerous to the self precisely because he is equipped by beauty to invade it, because he may not remain quite "other" enough.

> And he has beauty also,
> it's distressing ...
> a crouching mythological monster.

The "beauty" in "Marriage" seems always to be crouching and waiting for a chance to break in and overwhelm the careful cerebrations, the witty satire, the pure descriptions, in short, all the defensive maneuvers, the silences, the necessary restraints.

In *The Philosophy of Literary Form*, Kenneth Burke assures us that when you begin to consider the situations behind the tactics of expression, you will find tactics that organize a work technically *because* they organize it emotionally.... Hence, if you look for a man's *burden, you will* find the principle that reveals the structure of his unburdening, or in attenuated form, if you look for his problem, you will find the lead that explains the structure of his solution.[2]

The burden of the poem "Marriage" is one with the witty confusions (read confusions) of style in the poem. The poet, in presenting her broad subject in a way that is so willfully confusing, is also stipulating a kind of solitude. The woman of "multiple consciousness" defies "psychology" to explain her abilities.

> Psychology which explains everything
> explains nothing
> and we are still in doubt.

She should like to be alone. It is possible that in solitude the poet finds the complexity of consciousness, and its ability to change energy states like an excited electron, less frightening. "In the Days of Prismatic Color" is a poem that considers the fine clarity of the world "when Adam was alone." Alone he is able to perceive things clearly and with no obscurity, as a green thought in a green shade perhaps. The entrance of Eve is not an explicit event in this poem, but we are made to know that when Adam's solitude was lost, so was his uncomplicated vision. Admit the presence of an "other," explain or try to explain yourself and exactly how you see things, and all becomes complex, obscure.

The obscurity in Marianne Moore's vision of marriage lies in attempted explanations that are highly personal and shared only through "efforts of affection" not quite *equal to* affection. The obscurity, the single self con fronting another with marriage in mind, says to the reader in each unprepared-for leap of sensibility, "*I* should like to be alone." But here *we* are, and the poem, pulled in the direction of silence by its desire for solitude and unapproachability, is acknowledging us in every image restrainfully given over to language. It is also daring us to make at least equal efforts of affection on its behalf. It is an effort of communication, an uncomfortable one. Nevertheless, in that discomfort is a real truth about the human predicament. We can never have the occasional comfort of affection, of the beautiful image that strikes love in us, without the pain of reaching out, offering something too personal for words, in words, in other words, and in yet other words.

NOTE

2. Kenneth Burke, *The Philosophy of Literary Form* (New York: Vintage, 1957), p. 77.

—Pamela White Hadas. *Marianne Moore: Poet of Affection* (Syracuse: Syracuse University Press, 1977): 144–147.

LAURENCE STAPLETON ON THE ORIGINS OF IDEAS

[Laurence Stapleton is the author of *Some Poets and Their Resources: The Future Agenda: Lawrence, Emerson, Heaney, Bishop, Muir, Thomas, Melville, Wilbur,* and *Marianne Moore: The Poet's Advance.* Here, the author uncovers the origins of many of Moore's ideas about marriage.]

Taken as a whole, "Marriage" is unlike any other piece by her. Its brilliance is set off by a faceting that prevents the reader from looking at the center of poetic energy. One ventures the guess that "Marriage" comes close to a roman a clef in verse, and had special meanings for particular readers that can only be more abstractly glimpsed by later ones. Both the reading and conversation notebooks show a preoccupation with this subject in the early New York years. One conversation with Stieglitz is set down in some detail. He spoke of the lack of understanding between him and his first wife; that he married her because he was told that she expected him to. "So one day I woke up and found that I was married.... Now she blames me for the very thing that she married me for.... She said to me you are only fit to be a lover. Well why shouldn't I be a lover? If a married man must stop being a lover the moment he is married there is something wrong w[ith] the institution."[27] The poem begins "This institution"—a rare example of Marianne Moore's placing the object of a sentence first—and it is likely that the term stayed in her mind after these touchingly frank disclosures by Stieglitz.

More immediately in the background of the poem was the widespread discussion of Bryher's marriage to Robert McAlmon in 1921. Mrs. Moore and Marianne had invited them to tea in February with Scofield Thayer and Sibley Watson. A letter to "Badger" described the occasion. "The girls arrived at about twenty past. Hilda had just had time before the men came, to say that W. had been married to 'Robert' a little while before and that that had made them late. The girls looked lovely and the men were graciousness and responsiveness itself but what an earthquake."[28]

Two months later, when Marianne Moore was having dinner with Thayer, he gave her a clipping from the *New York Times* about the wedding. The headline was "'Heiress' Writer Weds Village Poet" and the account stressed Greenwich Village gossip about the reported proposal of the wealthy Miss Winifred Ellerman, who had taken the *nom de plume*, Bryher, to the impecunious bohemian Robert McAlmon. Marianne refused to see anything humorous in the newspaper story, and said that she found the marriage anything but romantic. Whereupon Thayer asked if it was unromantic to be married on Valentine's Day.[29] A number of their friends believed that he wished to marry Marianne;[30] doubtless he was not alone in this hope. Circumstances like these account for the turbulence of the early drafts of the poem and the current of emotion that sustains its high comedy when perfected. No one seems to me to have read it with better understanding than William Carlos Williams. "Of marriage there is no solution in the poem and no attempt at a solution; nor is there an attempt to shirk thought about it," he wrote in 1924.[31] In the same article he arrived at the principle that I believe a modern reader can only endorse: "The interstices for the light and not the interstitial web of thought concerned her.... Thus the material is as the handling: the thought, the word, the rhythm—all in the style. The effect is in the penetration of the light itself; how much how little; the appearance of the luminous background.[32]

NOTES

27. Rosenbach 1250/23, p. 59.
28. MM to JWM, February 20, 1921.
29. MM to JWM, April 4, 1921.
30. See William Carlos Williams, *Autobiography*.
31. "Marianne Moore," *Dial*, 78 (1925), 399.
32. Ibid.

> —Laurence Stapleton. *Marianne Moore: The Poet's Advance* (Princeton: Princeton University Press, 1978): 40–42.

ELIZABETH PHILLIPS ON MOORE'S USE OF COLLAGE AS A VEHICLE FOR HUMOR

[Elizabeth Phillips is a Professor Emerita of English at Wake Forest University. She has written three books of criticism, *Emily Dickinson: Personae and Performance*, *Marianne Moore*, and *Edgar Allen Poe: An American Imagination*. In this section, Phillips claims that Moore's choice of the collage medium aids in the humor of the piece.]

An interest in design and pattern was an aid in Moore's mastery of the problems that arise from a vision of the complexities of knowledge and perception, of being too much conscious and conscious of too much, as F. R. Leavis observed of T. S. Eliot's poem *The Wasteland* (1922). Moore's work in "several" voices. *Marriage* (1923), like *The Wasteland*, is without narrative continuity and takes its form from the collage in which diverse fragments are assembled without a center of gravity. The longest of her experimental compositions, it is in free verse.

Its simplest antecedent is a quatrain she published in 1915 as a "found" poem, "Counseil to a Bacheler":

If thou bee younge, then marie not yett;
If thou bee olde, then no wyfe gett;

For younge mens' wyves will not be taught,
And olde mens' wyves bee good for naught.

She indicated that the *verse trouvé* was an "Elizabethan Trencher motto—Bodleian Library [with title and modification of second line]." Never reprinted, it is the first instance of Moore's habit of preserving lines or expressions that she liked. After the fun she had in giving her own title to the quatrain, touching it up, and publishing it under her signature, she began to use quotations sparingly but inventively in many of her poems. (...)

Marriage is an assemblage of which Moore said, "I was just making a note of some things I'd come on that took my fancy-either the phrasing or the sound," "words that I didn't want to lose.... and I put them together as plausibly as I could."[7] It would have been no exaggeration for her to have said "hilariously" or "wittily" instead of "plausibly." She tried to be helpful without being immodest or giving herself away. She questioned whether or not *Marriage* was a poem and insisted that it was not a theory of marriage at all, "doesn't even approach it." Given a large number of disparate and conflicting elements in a collage, the form is a precarious contrivance. The elements tend to carry on guerilla warfare with one another, and the arrangement incurs the risk of seeming impenetrably chaotic or of being arbitrary rather than unified. Whether Moore intended it or not—and I suspect she did—the collage becomes appropriately witty for the subject of marriage, its tensions, disharmonies, and irreconcilables. (Picasso, as one of the originators of the collage, or synthetic cubism [1912–1914], understood the humorous possibilities of the form.) The attitude of the poet and the tones of the many voices in *Marriage* as text plus the incongruities of the texts beyond the text should allay some of the criticism of readers who have not enjoyed the esprit with which Moore views a paradise lost. (...)

It is, however, Moore who is responsible for the wit implicit in the arrangement. The woman's expression reveals other possible, conceivable attitudes, such as her confident assumption of the right to speak, pleasure in ridiculing man, and grudging admiration for him. There are women who would not give him the time of day, or night, and there are women who would not protest so energetically. The poet is known for the axiom in "Silence" (1924): "The deepest feeling always shows itself in silence; / not in silence, but restraint." In *Marriage*, restraint is not synonymous with Adam's constraint.

NOTE

7. Grace Shulman, "Conversation with Marianne Moore," *Quarterly Review of Literature*, 16 (1969), pp. 159–160. Other comments on *Marriage* appear in the Foreword to *A Marianne Moore Reader*, p. xv.

—Elizabeth Phillips. *Marianne Moore*. (New York: Frederick Ungar Publishing Company, 1982): 44, 45–46, 49.

TAFFY MARTIN ON THE NEGATIVITY IN "MARRIAGE"

[Taffy Martin teaches at the University of Poitiers. She is the author of several critical articles works, *Marianne Moore: Subversive Modernist* among them. In this extract, Martin comments on the unusual negativity present in the poem.]

Wrong from the start, then, any attempt at marriage, "this amalgamation which can never be more / than an interesting impossibility," will be doomed to failure. Moore's criticism has been impartially distributed since each participant in the union shares the same faults. Her attack becomes even more successful because she reinforces this impartiality with relentless dispassion. The poem offers neither a death blow nor an alternative to the institution but a depressing version of half success. The partners are sentenced to "cycloid inclusiveness," a "striking grasp of opposites / opposed each to the other, not to unity...." Moore's argument that there can be no respite in this struggle intensifies throughout the poem until she asks a question to which she already knows the answer.

What can one do for them—
these savages
condemned to disaffect
all those who are not visionaries
alert to undertake the silly task
of making people noble? (68)

Since nothing can be done to aid the self-deluded, Moore ruthlessly concludes that this naive but mistaken belief in the efficacy of "public promises ... to fulfill a private obligation" dictates that "the statesmanship / of an archaic Daniel Webster / persists to their simplicity of temper / as the essence of the matter." Meaningless contradiction, a passive symbol of church or state, and the withdrawal of personal contact close the poem and become Moore's enigmatic representation of "the essence of the matter."

'Liberty and union
now and forever';
the Book on the writing-table;
the hand in the breast-pocket," (70)

One can claim to be attempting liberty and union, but the combination is a farce. A book on a writing table may block as many thoughts as it inspires, and if the capitalization in "Book" signifies the Bible, a book Marianne Moore certainly knew well, the passive image is even more damaging. A hand in the breast pocket cannot offer to shake another nor can it signal any other traditional pledge of disarmament. The posture is unequivocally closed and defensive. The institution has been dismissed. The issue is closed.

"Marriage" is an unusual poem in the Moore canon because its treatment is more openly personal than that of most of her poems. More important, Moore's treatment of passion, confusion, and deluded vision is undeniably negative. The fact that her sensuous language vividly captures the attraction of one party to another only intensifies the shock of the rest of the poem. In most poems, Moore treats such confusion and deluded vision as positive qualities, as opportunities for wordplay or enjoyment.

> —Taffy Martin. *Marianne Moore: Subversive Modernist* (Austin: University of Texas Press, 1986): 23–24.

BERNARD F. ENGEL ON LIBERTY THROUGH SELF-DISCIPLINE

[In this portion of the essay, Engel expounds on liberty through self-discipline as per Moore's technique and Webster's quote.]

One of several qualities novices lack is the discipline that not only is an important value in Moore's ethics but also is frequently her subject for a poem. The paradox that liberty may be bred by self-discipline, a restraint in action and expression, is explored in the long poem "Marriage." The tone is somewhat humorous, sympathetic yet at times mockingly ironic; the strategy, unusual for Moore but appropriate in this poem, includes a report of an imagined dialogue between an Adam and Eve who are not so much the characters of the Garden of Eden as representatives of married woman and man. The lines are fairly short, usually six to eight syllables; lines of twelve or more syllables are usually followed by lines of four or five. The tone, the mixture of dialogue and speculation, and the brief line allow variety and much wit and paradox.

After an opening passage of seventeen lines commenting on the seriousness of marriage and pondering what the original Adam and Eve might think of the institution by now, longer passages introduce an Adam and Eve of the present, struggling with the human complexities that, the poem says, psychology cannot explain. Eve is talented, changeable, and is said (in lines reminiscent of Robinson Jeffers, the only such passage in Moore's published work) to be possessed of an almost suicidal beauty. This reflection leads to recollection of her role as "the central flaw" in Eden—as the cause of "that lamentable accident" that exempted Adam from primary blame for man's loss of the

Garden, an exemption Moore as a woman makes a point of referring to with sarcasm. Like Eve, Adam has a beauty that, the poem tells us, is properly celebrated in certain works of art. Adam has been a prophet and sage; but he has failed to observe the unpredictable qualities of woman, he has taken an undue pride in the reverence some have paid him, and he has let himself be dazzled into marriage, a state that is a "trivial" source for the disruption of the grand role he has enjoyed.

Once married, a couple finds that the counsels of Hymen, the marriage god, will be of no help. For example, his advice that marriage late in life is best is of little aid to those who presumably have wed at the customary age. Man and wife must recognize that friction is to be expected and perhaps even valued, for it is a way of testing experience; they must learn at some pain the difference between independence and bondage, and they must accept inevitable differences in opinion and in desires. There follows a dialogue between Eve and Adam, each presenting favorite accusations against the other. The conversation ends with the speaker's comment that each loves himself rather too much and that they are "poor" as long as this is true—poor, we may deduce, in peace and in the strength a better understanding of each other could give them.

The concluding issue is stated in the inquiry as to what can be done for such "savages" who frustrate all but the most visionary of those who would like to help them. It is obviously rare that a marriage joins two whole-souled opposites who instead of feuding can reinforce each other. Indeed, so ideal a marriage is so unlikely that the possibility of it is for a moment mocked in lines comparing it to Columbus demonstration with the egg. Yet, though improbable, such a "charitive Euroclydon," such an impersonal though passionate love, is still the ideal; it would develop a "disinterestedness" that "the world" hates but may nevertheless be found in those with "simplicity of temper." An example appears in an old-fashioned wedding picture. The photographed couple's sturdy individualism of pose, obvious simplicity, and forthright reliance on principle (indicated by a Bible in the foreground) illustrate that paradox verified, so to speak, in the closing lines by allusion to Daniel Webster's paradox that we must somehow in marriage, as elsewhere, respect and win both liberty and union. The political allusion serves to give one statement application not only to the marriage partnership but to life generally. We must somehow unite in our lives a proper care for the physical with a due recognition for the spiritual in all experience.

"Marriage" is atypical in dealing with an intangible circumstance that Moore could not effectively represent by means of an object or an animal. Possibly because of her "restraint," her desire to keep herself out of the situation, she set down her details with so little explanation that several passages are elliptical. The poem lacks the intensity of, for example, parts of George Meredith's "Modern Love" series; such intensity, however, might be out of place in what is essentially a witty, ironically pitying commentary. In such later poems on the theme of self-discipline as "What Are Years?" and "Nevertheless" Moore becomes more directly editorial. The subjects in these poems, however, are simpler. "Marriage" is complex at least partly because the relationships it discusses are complex.

—Bernard F. Engel. *Marianne Moore, Revised Edition* (Boston: Twayne Publishers, 1989): 52–54.

JEREDITH MERRIN ON MOORE'S DECENTERING OF TRADITIONAL MODES OF POWER

[Jeredith Merrin is a Professor of English at Ohio State University. She is the author of *Shift* and *Bat Ode*, books of poems, and *Marianne Moore, Elizabeth Bishop, and the Uses of Tradition*, a critical examination. Here, she explains Moore's methods of de-centering power as a part of her feminism.]

A few more observations may illustrate how both Moore and Bishop undercut male pomposity and imperiousness, deploring the fact (as Moore put it in "Marriage") "that men have power / and sometimes one is made to feel it." That power may be in the form of a boorish "man looking into the sea, "or of "monopolists / of 'stars, garters, buttons / and other shining baubles'"

("Marriage"); in the form of preening, combative roosters, or of rapacious sixteenth-century conquistadors, tramping through the South American jungle (and stalking native women) to the tune of *"L'Homme armé"* ("Brazil, January 1, 1502"). Everywhere, their poetry implicitly supports the moral assertion that under no conditions is a woman's identity or fate to be considered less significant than that of a man. (As just a few obvious examples, see Moore's "Sojourn in the Whale" or "Paper Nautilus," Bishop's "Filling Station" or "In the Waiting Room.") Whether through satiric jabs or subtle subversions of androcentric tropes, through serious development of subjects that have generally not been treated seriously by male poets, or simply through purposeful attention to their own metaphysical dilemmas and observations, these poets repeatedly cause us to recognize that a woman's spiritual experience is every bit as much "at the center," and as representative, as a man's.

But only *as much* at the center. If, as I would argue, both Moore and Bishop overturn the long-standing cultural assumption that males somehow exist at the center of reality and females at the periphery, they do not then assert a "gynocentricity" equal and opposite to male "phallocentricity." What I think particularly large and important about these women poets, besides their extraordinary talent, is their thoroughgoing (if sometimes subtle) resistance to all *forms* of egocentricity and domination. Rather than relying on the central, self-exposed and often self-congratulatory "I," they make room for multiple and juxtaposed perspectives—both human and nonhuman—reminding us that no matter what position we occupy there is always, as Emily Dickinson asserted, "Another—way to see."

Consider, for example, the way that Marianne Moore (who was "not," in her own words, "matrimonially ambitious") credits views and accommodates voices other than her own through her habit of frequent quotation—as here, in her evocation of a hypothetical Adam's experience of sexual desire and of the institution of "Marriage":

Unnerved by the nightingale
and dazzled by the apple,
impelled by "the illusion of a fire

effectual to extinguish fire,"
compared with which
the shining of the earth
is but deformity—a fire
"as high as deep
as bright as broad
as long as life itself,"
he stumbles over marriage,
"a very trivial object indeed"
to have destroyed the attitude
in which he stood—
the ease of the philosopher
unfathered by a woman.

Or consider the way that Moore's poems often remain delicately poised between two contradictory points of view. We see, for example, in the sea-scrubbed New England coastal town of "The Steeple Jack" an ambiguous Eden—at once pristine and slightly sinister; in the elaborate Louis Fifteenth candelabrum of "No Swan So Fine" an example of the double-edged victory and vain-glory of artifice; in the historically rich and naturally lush state of Virginia ("Virginia Britannia") evidence at once of breathtaking democratic diversity and deplorable imperialist arrogance.

—Jeredith Merrin. *An Enabling Humility: Marianne Moore, Elizabeth Bishop and the Uses of Tradition* (New Brunswick: Rutgers University Press, 1990): 138–40.

CHARLES MOLESWORTH ON THE POEM AS A MODERNIST EXERCISE IN PERSPECTIVE

[Charles Molesworth is a Professor of English at Queens College, CUNY. He is the author of books of both poetry and criticism, *Marianne Moore: A Literary Life* among them. In this chapter, he explains the poem as a modernist exercise on perspective.]

Such a nervous hiding of the real subject, or at least her feelings about it, is in part a noticeable feature of "Marriage," as many have observed. Moore herself further hides the subject when she argues, as a note in the *Complete Poems*, that the poem is only a collection of "statements that took my fancy which I tried to arrange plausibly." Yet in an undated letter of 1923, she specifically told Warner that she was hoping to give offense by the poem, especially to those people who too casually assumed that marriage was not a permanent state. But the poem doesn't give offense, largely because it presents so many different attitudes toward marriage. Other letters in 1923 indicate that Moore was increasingly unhappy with the work of many of her contemporaries. Her mother quotes her to Warner as saying that there wasn't anything in *Broom* she couldn't do without, whereas she felt the opposite about the *Spectator* and the magazines she read about natural history. In the same letter Mrs. Moore expressed her and her daughter's view that obscenity was acceptable only if it were subordinate to the worth of the entire work. Moore herself vowed to go to *Broom* with her work only to spite Gorham Munson and Kenneth Burke. This was a dig at Munson's new magazine, *Secession*, which he and Burke were editing, and which Munson polemically presented as better and more advanced than all the other magazines. In fact, Munson included negative appraisals of other journals in early issues, singling out *The Dial*, among others. In the middle of February, Glenway Wescott quoted William Carlos Williams as having said, after Moore left the room, "I am in perfect terror of Marianne," and at the party he had said, when reading his poems, "I have to leave some out, because I could not say such words before Marianne Moore."

It was, somewhat ironically, Wescott for whom Moore was busy at work on "Marriage," as early as April, 1923. Mrs. Moore liked Monroe Wheeler a lot, so much so that she reported to Warner that they agreed to call him "Monroe." Wescott was another matter, however. By the beginning of 1924 Mrs. Moore confessed to Warner that they didn't care for Wescott anymore, but tolerated him for Wheeler's sake. She specifically objected to Wescott's novel then being serialized in *The Dial*, and felt bad that Moore's review of Stevens had to be in the same issue. In May, 1923, Wheeler and Wescott had both told Moore and her mother that they were going to model their lives after the two women and give up literary celebrities. But apparently Wescott's resolution was not to last; among other things, he returned from a trip abroad with news of Pound (he was now sporting a pointed beard), and that Thayer was on the outs with several people for rejecting Mina Loy's essay on Gertrude Stein for *The Dial*.

Nevertheless, in the midst of all this literary jockeying, Moore worked steadily on "Marriage," and was able to show Wescott and Wheeler at least a rough draft by the end of April. By the third week of May, Wescott had prepared a "dummy" to send to the printer in Germany, and he shows it to Moore. The poem was finally printed, as a chapbook, by Wheeler's Manikin Press, appearing late in 1923, in an edition of about 200 copies, mostly for presentation. In several copies there was laid in the two-page essay on Moore's poetry written by Wescott and later used, in a revised form, in *The Dial*. Wescott and Wheeler both took delight in telling Moore that Thayer, when he saw the book, "went white," apparently with surprise. So the poem that Moore hoped would give offense to many served at first only as a focus of envious competition.

Still the outstanding irony is that this self-effacing poet who never married wrote her longest poem on a subject that was controversial, timely, and apparently irresolvable. In what is almost a series of musical riffs or movements, the poem is built largely on quotations, though no more so than "An Octopus." It is a classic example of the modernist poem as an exercise in perspectivalism, shifting its tone, its vocabulary, and its point of view frequently and often without notice. The poetic sequence, so often resorted to by modernist poets, might have been a more "comfortable" format for what Moore wanted to say, but for whatever the reasons and the consequences, the poem proceeds—at least typographically—in one uninterrupted flow. The opening, with its self-conscious correction:

> This institution,
> perhaps one should say enterprise
> out of respect for which
> one says one need not change one's mind
> about a thing one has believed in,

requiring public promises
of one's intention
to fulfil a private obligation....

has enough of a mix of an apparent attempt at honesty ("perhaps one should say") and a still evasive tone ("one says one ...") to indicate that the lyric impulse will be folding back on itself in complex ways. The poem does have moments of celebration and anguish, even of humor and biting satire, but if it were expected to deliver a final answer, or even a definitive but subjective opinion, about the worth or desirability of the married state, such a definitive formulation is itself clearly called into question:

Psychology which
explains everything explains nothing,
and we are still in doubt.

Not only do we hear Adam on Eve, and Eve on Adam, but any number of authorities are cited, in such profusion that one could imagine that Moore was gently satirizing authority itself, as Chaucer did with his Wife of Bath, also an expert manipulator of cited wisdom on the subject of the relations between the sexes.

NOTES

For Kreymborg, see his memoir, *Troubador*, New York: Boni & Liveright, 1925. Alyse Gregory tells her version in *The Day Is Gone*, New York: E. P. Dutton, 1948, while Llewlyn Powys' memoir of this period is *The Verdict of Bridlegoose*, New York: Harcourt, Brace, 1926. The fictionalized account of an evening with Moore and her mother is part of Robert McAlmon's *Post-Adolescence*, Dijon: Contact Editions, n.d. Two other memoirs supplied incidental details: Richard Aldington, *Life for Life's Sake: A Book of Reminiscences*, New York: Viking, 1941, and Robert McAlmon (with supplementary chapters by Kay Boyle), *Being Geniuses Together*, New York: Doubleday, 1968. Bryher's memories are recorded in *The Heart to Artemis: A Writer's Memoirs*, London: Collins, 1963. Background information is from Frederick Hoffman, *The Twenties*, New York: The Free Press, 1962, and Allen Churchill, *The Improper Bohemians*, New York: E. P. Dutton, 1959. Additional information on the literary scene was taken from Gorham Munson's *The Awakening Twenties*, Baton Rouge: Louisiana State U. Press, 1985. Historical data were taken from Henry Steele Commager, *The American Mind*, New Haven: Yale U. Press, 1950, and from Henry May, *The End of American Innocence: A Study of the First Years of Our Time, 1912–1917*, New

York: Alfred Knopf, 1959. Some details about Mina Loy and Lola Ridge came from William Drake, *The First Wave: Women Poets in America, 1915–1945*, New York: Macmillan, 1987.

Information about the Zorachs was drawn from *Marguerite and William Zorach: The Cubist Years, 1915–1918*, by Marilyn Friedman Hoffman, Hanover, N.H.: University Press of New England, 1987. Alfred Stieglitz is the subject of *America and Alfred Stieglitz: A Collective Portrait*, ed. Waldo Frank, et al., New York: Doubleday, Doran, 1934.

Professor Donald Miller, of the History Department at Lafayette College, shared his wide-ranging bibliographical knowledge with me, as well as a typescript of his biography of Lewis Mumford.

—Charles Molesworth. *Marianne Moore: A Literary Life* (New York: Atheneum, 1990): 186–188.

Darlene Williams Erickson on Collage, Materials, and Organization

[Darlene Williams Erickson is a Professor of English at Ohio Dominican University. She is the author of many scholarly articles, a distinguished teacher and the author of *Illusion Is More Precise Than Precision*. Here, she discusses Moore's use of materials and organization in her collage poem.]

After a careful first reading, most readers can follow what Hartman described as Moore's "gossip on the baroque scale." She does indeed seem to have "arranged plausibly" in a kind of conversation almost everything one has always wanted to know about marriage, capsuling her collection of phrases with the disclaimer,

> Everything to do with love is a mystery;
> it is more than a day's work
> to investigate this science.

At first the catalogue of 289 lines seems random, only vaguely associative, but in fact, the dialectic is meticulously woven. Moore frequently claimed that she despised connectives, at least connectives in the obvious sense. In order to see this montage as a whole, the reader must learn to participate in and to enjoy the anthology—without the connecting links most poets provide. One idea merely melts into another, without transitions. (Moore once wrote, "I myself ... would rather be told too little than too much.")[35] In "Marriage" Moore is assuming that the discriminating reader shares her predilection.

Once again, it is William Carlos Williams who offers a useful critical tool for dealing with the text. In "A Novelette and Other Prose, 1921–1931," Williams wrote of Moore:

> A course in mathematics would not be wasted on a poet, or a reader of poetry, if he remember no more from it than the intersection of loci: from all angles lines converging and crossing establish points. He might carry it further and say in his imagination that apprehension perforates at places, through to understanding—as white is at the intersection of blue and green and yellow and red. It is this white light that is the background of all good work.... The intensification of desire toward this purity is the modern variant. It is that which interests me most and seems most solid among the qualities I witness in my contemporaries; it is a quality present in much or even all that Miss Moore does.[36]

Later, in 1948 in the *Quarterly Review of Literature*, he reiterates that point: "Therefore Miss Moore has taken recourse to the mathematic of art. Picasso does no different: a portrait is a stratagem singularly related to a movement among the means of the craft."[37]

Williams also calls Moore's "Marriage" an "anthology of transit,"[38] meaning that one must allow all of Moore's directions, insights, tones, quotations, and epigrams—her "crazy quilt," in Hartman's parlance—to move and to intersect. Through the intersection of ideas, one comes to appreciate the profound complexity of one of life's great-enigmas, the interaction of one human being with another in the enterprise called marriage. The poem does not precisely "mean" anything. It is instead a conversation, a comprehensive dialectic based upon some of the greatest myths, motifs, symbols, visions, and commentaries on the subject of marriage. It passes no judgment, solves no problems. If, as Doris Lessing has said, people are "hungry for answers, not hungry for ways of thinking toward problems," they will be disappointed.[39] If they are willing to search for truths in the interstices, in the intersections of loci, they will learn a great deal from Moore's "little anthology of phrases [she] did not want to lose."

In "Feeling and Precision," Moore wrote, "Feeling at its deepest—as we all have reason to know—tends to be inarticulate."[40] And that is an important "mathematical" principle in "Marriage." Although the poem is replete with the deepest of human emotions, the intersections of emotional loci occur with such disarming precision that the reader must remain attentive to find them. Taffy Martin has argued that the voice here and in other poems remains deadpan, that it does not seem to convey grand emotions. In such a stance, Martin feels, Moore creates a music particularly suitable for the twentieth century.[41] One might argue instead that there are *many* voices in the poem and that they are not all deadpan. Sometimes the voice is that of the poet summarizing or synthesizing, but many times the voices are anonymous presenters of information, much of it ready-made from the past. In the intersection of the many voices, which speak but do not always, hear, lies real poignancy and intense emotion, but emotion so deep that it tends to seem inarticulate. (...)

"Marriage" is a very effective poem, at least for those readers who, as T. S. Eliot had suggested, "are willing and accustomed to take a little trouble over poetry." Moore's success in "Marriage" occurs in part because she has turned to her cabinet of fossils, her "flies in amber," to pull off the shelves of her prodigious memory many different perceptions about the complexities of marriage. Sometimes the found objects, the objets trouvés, are lines that caught her fancy merely because of what they said or the way they said it. Some references carry the baggage of their stories (Diana, Ecclesiasticus, Ahasuerus, Hercules), while others are treasured primarily for their unique beauty ("something feline, / something colubrine," or "treading chasms / on the uncertain footing of a spear"). Perhaps reflecting some of the theories of Marcel Duchamp, Moore is suggesting that the important thing about a phrase is not that it is original but instead that she, as artist, chose it and placed it in a setting of her making. For the poem occurs, as William Carlos Williams has suggested, not in the originality of the materials but instead in what Moore does with them as she moves ideas and images along lines that will intersect and come alive in polyphonic conversations in the reader's mind. Sometimes the intersection produces laughter; sometimes it offers the most profound sadness. But it is this multiplication, this quickening, this burrowing through and blasting aside in which the poem happens. It is at the intersection of images and ideas that the white light of freshness and new insight really occurs. Moore was confident enough, and humble enough, to understand that she had to use the same materials as others before her. There was no need for pretense. Originality lay in edging ideas against one another in brilliantly novel ways.

NOTES

35. Moore, "Humility, Concentration, and Gusto," p. 15.
36. Williams, *Selected Essays*, p. 122.
37. Ibid., p. 293.
38. Ibid., p. 123.
39. Quoted in Gallagher, "Throwing the Scarecrows from the Garden," p. 52.
40. Moore, "Feeling and Precision," p. 3.
41. Taffy Martin, *Marianne Moore: Subversive Modernist* (Austin: University of Texas Press, 1986), p. 132.

> —Darlene Williams Erickson. *Illusion is More Precise Than Precision: The Poetry of Marianne Moore* (Tuscaloosa: The University of Alabama Press, 1992.): 102–104, 112.

BRUCE HENDERSON ON FEMINISM AND RHETORIC

[Bruce Henderson is the author of "The 'Eternal Eve' and the 'Newly Born Woman': Voices, Performance, and Marianne Moore's 'Marriage.'" In this essay, Henderson engages the poem as a part of a feminist rhetoric.]

In the first sentence of "Marriage," Marianne Moore describes this "enterprise" as "requiring public promises / of one's intention / to fulfill a private obligation" (*Complete Poems* 62). Her wording immediately suggests at least an element of criticism of the verbal performances associated with the wedding ceremony: the contrast between public and private acts, traceable throughout her writings, is one the poet herself felt keenly. This is not merely a contrast between negative and positive qualities; rather, Moore seems more concerned with determining the ethical appropriateness of a situation. The public act of promising, she seems to be saying, is finally neither a guarantee that either party will fulfill the private obligation, nor is it the most authentic or sincere forum for such a statement of commitment.

The lines also suggest a second set of contrasts, and again these are neither hard and fast nor purely definitive: the typical gender associations of public performances versus private ones. In "Marriage," Adam is more often than not cast as the orator, the public speaker, while Eve is more at home in the world of conversation, a witty, sometimes artificial (in both the most and least pejorative senses of that word) conversation, not unlike that of an Enlightenment salon. Although, as we will see, both characters venture into other realms of spoken discourse, Moore fairly consistently schematizes them.

In this linkage of masculine to public speaking and feminine to "interpersonal" or "poetic" communication, Moore looks ahead to contemporary French feminist theories associated with the psychoanalytic theories of Lacan and the deconstructive sorties of Derrida. Hélène Cixous, who in some ways represents the interests of both these major thinkers, differentiates between typical masculine and feminine responses to the acts of speaking and writing. Here she refers to women's resistance to oratory:

> Every woman has known the torture of beginning to speak aloud, heart beating as if to break, occasionally falling into loss of language ... because for woman speaking—even just opening her mouth—in public is something rash, a transgression.... We are not culturally accustomed to speaking ... employing the suitable rhetoric.... The orator is asked to unwind a small thread, dry and taut. We like uneasiness, questioning. (92–93)

Contemporary specialists in gender and communication theory might take issue with some of Cixous' generalizations, but it is true that the history of women has more often than not kept them out of the traditional public forums for rhetoric, and "relegated" (from a patriarchal point of view) them to the more informal (that is, invisible) worlds of kitchen and schoolroom. This is also often true in the representation of women in literature. A St. Joan is such a *rara avis*, both historically and dramatically, because she is a public speaker.

Eve is the first speaker introduced in the poem (that is, after the narrator, who is either female, in keeping with the implied lyric association of the poet and her poem, or neuter), and she is praised for her linguistic ability:

> able to write simultaneously
> in three languages—
> English, German, and French—
> and talk in the meantime.
>   (*Complete Poems* 62)

Eve is the writer in the poem (perhaps she is also the writer of the poem?), but her talents extend beyond the mere ability to compose sentences. She is also a polyglot (whereas Adam appears only to speak English, and the King's English at that), and a modern one, schooled in the three primary languages of twentieth-century scholarship: indeed, she might bypass many a contemporary Ph.D. in the humanities in this respect.

Not only this, but Eve is able to "talk in the meantime," suggesting both a superior mind and the traditional female dilemma of having to do more than one thing at a time: the image of the wife or mother who must tend house and do her "own" work of the mind simultaneously. Her first words are telling: "I should like to be alone." These are not the words of the rhetorician, but the blunt, declarative statement of the woman demanding a "room of one's own." Though Eve participates in rhetorical discourse throughout the poem, it is clear that language fulfills two principal functions for her: it is either a way of ordering her own experience of the world (a primarily poetic function) or a way of stating her needs and desires (here an essentially expressive function). Language and its enactment in performance are not, for Eve, strategies for persuasion; rather they allow her to maintain that sense of "unease" and "questioning" Cixous sees as the core of what she and other theorists call *l'écriture féminine* translated variously as "feminine writing" or "discourse of women."

Eve holds her own in the more traditionally rhetorical performances in the poem. Much of the last third of the poem consists of an exchange between Adam and Eve, an exchange that is somewhere between formal debate and heated discussion, initiated by Adam's critique of Eve's body, specifically her hair— "What monarch would not blush / to have a wife / with hair like a shaving-brush?" (*Complete Poems* 67). Her stylistically balanced but fierce responses to Adam's witty and wounding remarks are frequently composed of lists, rather than of arguments *per se,* and the objects in the lists are often connected through poetic inference, metaphoric and metonymic qualities, such as "Men are monopolists / of 'stars, garters, buttons / and other shining baubles.'" Similarly, in her response to Adam's definition of a "wife" as a "coffin" (these lines quoted, by the way, from Ezra Pound, one of Moore's closest friends and most respected peers), Eve questions, both rhetorically and existentially,

.... This butterfly,
this waterfly, this nomad
that has 'proposed
to settle on my hand for life'—
What can one do with it? (*Complete Poems* 68)

Eve moves progressively from one species of fragile insect to another to the final and damning "nomad" in her need to name the creature who is both her lover and enemy. The question she asks is perhaps in part a rhetorical one, not requiring a specific, uttered response, but it is also a real and serious dilemma for Eve: where and how to fit man into her lexicon and into her life?

—Bruce Henderson. "The 'Eternal Eve' and the 'Newly Born Woman': Voices, Performance, and Marianne Moore's 'Marriage.'" *Images of the Self as Female: The Achievement of Women*

Artists in Re-envisioning Feminine Identity. Eds. Kathryn N Benzel and Lauren Pringle De La Vars (Lewiston: The Edwin Mellen Press, 1992): pp. 122–124.

JEANNE HEUVING ON "MARRIAGE" AS A CRITIQUE OF PATRIARCHAL HIERARCHY

[Jeanne Heuving is an Associate Professor of English at the University of Washington at Bothell. She has published *Omissions Are Not Accidents: Gender in the Art of Marianne Moore.* In this essay, Heuving sees the poem as a critique of patriarchal hierarchy and the inequity of power between genders.]

Although Moore is intrigued by this institution/enterprise that is more than she can express it to be, and is appreciative of certain aspects of it, "Marriage" forms a powerful critique of this central institution of patriarchy and of male and female roles within it.[19] While this poem discloses the imbalance of power between men and women within marriage, it also establishes the forms of thinking and representation that make this imbalance possible: "that striking grasp of opposites / opposed each to the other, not to unity." While the few critics who have considered "Marriage" at any length typically have sought to sort out blame between Adam and Eve, such an approach misses the accomplishment of Moore's meditation on marriage as a "cycloid inclusiveness" in which the parts are defined by their relationship to each other.[20] If in many ways Moore is attracted to the nonsense of Marriage, she abhors its ill-reason—the occlusion of otherness by a forced and unreasoned unity. Moore, like Irigaray and others, is criticizing a hierarchical duality in which a privileged term absorbs the otherness of the secondary term under an ideal of unity or identity (of "the same"). Adam, as the privileged term, "loves himself so much, / he can permit himself / no rival in that love"; and Eve, as the suppressed term, "loves herself so much, / she cannot see her self enough." As egotist and narcissist, they are condemned to solitary confinement within an institution which, while based on their sexual difference, will not admit to any actual otherness.

The central myth around which "Marriage" forms is the story of Adam and Eve—the Adam and Eve, at least in part, of Milton's *Paradise Lost*. Although Moore conveys the grandeur and splendor of Milton's *Paradise Lost* in passages such as "Below the incandescent stars / below the incandescent fruit, / the strange experience of beauty; / its existence is too much," she also parodies his tragic argument—absorbing and deploying its epic grandeur Milton affirms the hierarchical order by describing Eve as "for Adam and the God in him," and in the passage in which Eve addresses Adam: "O thou for whom / And from whom I was form'd flesh of thy flesh, / And without whom am to no end, my Guide / and Head."[21] Moore subverts that hierarchy by introducing Eve into her poem first and referring to Adam as the visitor. Moore also converts Eve's respectful address into a comic epithet: "the O thou / to whom, from whom, / without whom nothing—Adam." She further subverts the Biblical and Miltonic versions of the story by providing Adam and Eve each with their own respective source of temptation: Hera's golden apples in the Hesperides and the snake. In neither case is the agony of temptation emphasized. Adam is quite simply bedazzled by the apple, "the illusion of a fire / effectual to extinguish fire," and Eve's relation to the snake is described as "that invaluable accident / exonerating Adam."

But if differences exist between Moore's and Milton's poems, Moore also borrows, and builds on, certain characteristics of Milton's Adam and Eve. Both Milton's and Moore's Adams possess language innately. In *Paradise Lost*, just after Adam's creation, he awakes to find himself endowed preternaturally with language:

> But who I was or where, or from what cause,
> Knew not; to speak I tri'd, and forthwith spake,
> My tongue obey'd and readily could name
> Whate'er I saw.[22]

Moore's Adam is blessed with the same immediate access to language, albeit comically:

> Alive with words,
> vibrating like a cymbal
> touched before it has been struck

Both Milton and Moore portray Eve as narcissistic. Milton's Eve describes her awakening from creation to Adam thus:

> The day I oft remember, when from sleep
> I first awak't, and found myself repos'd
> Under a shade on flow'rs, much wond'ring where
> And what I was, whence thither brought, and how,
> Not distant far from thence a murmuring sound
> Of waters issue'd from a Cave and spread
> Into a liquid Plain, then stood unmov'd
> Pure as th' expanse of Heav'n; I thither went
> With unexperienc't thought, and laid me down
> On the green bank, to look into the clear
> Smooth Lake, that to me seem'd another Sky.
> As I bent down to look, just opposite,
> A Shape within the wat'ry gleam appear'd
> Bending to look on me, I started back,
> It started back, but pleas'd I soon return'd,
> Pleas'd it returned as soon with answering looks
> Of sympathy and love: there I had fixt
> Mine eyes till now, and pin'd with vain desire,
> Had not a voice thus warned me, What thou seest,
> What there thou seest fair Creature is thyself
> With thee it came and goes: but follow me ...
>   what could I do,
> But follow straight, invisibly thus led?
> Till I espied thee fair indeed and tall,
> Under a Platan, yet methought less fair,
> Less winning soft, less amiably mild
> Than that smooth wat'ry image; back I turned.[23]

Emphasizing Eve's narcissistic qualities—"she cannot see herself enough"—Moore also portrays her as possessing an non-Adamic relation to language:

> able to write simultaneously
> in three languages—
> English, German and French
> and talk in the meantime;
> equally positive in demanding a commotion
> and in stipulating quiet.

Eve's relationship to language is characterized by multiplicity In fact, she may not be able to see herself enough because, unlike Adam, she does not possess a specular relation to language. According to Irigaray, women cannot be truly narcissistic, for their relation to language precludes a true narcissism. Consequently they come nearest to a language of their own self-affection when they engage in a contradictory or multiple expression, an écriture.

NOTES

19. Ostriker claims that "Marriage" "hides—under its elliptical surface—a rather absolute critique of patriarchy and its central institution" (*Stealing the Language*, 51). Lynn Keller and Cristanne Miller in "'the tooth of disputation:' Marianne Moore's 'Marriage,'" emphasize the "poet's deep ambivalence about the 'enterprise,' of marriage" (*Sagetrieb* 6, no. 3 [Winter 1987]: 100).

20. Stapleton remarks that Eve "in her various guises ... remains 'the central flaw / in that first crystal fine experiment'" (38). Keller and Miller maintain that "despite Moore's slightly more favorable portrait of the 'She,' both characters are repugnant in their viciousness and both are explicitly condemned for loving themselves too much" (110).

21. Milton, John, "Paradise Lost," *Complete Poems and Major Prose*, ed. Merritt Y. Hughes (Indianapolis: Odyssey Press, 1957), Chapter 4, lines 440–443.

22. Milton, Chapter 8, lines 270–273.

23. Milton, Chapter 4, lines 449–469, 475–480. Christine Froula claims that Eve is remembering an "origin innocent of patriarchal indoctrination, one whose resonances the covering trope of narcissism does not entirely suffice to control" ("When Eve Reads Milton: Undoing the Canonical Economy," *Critical Inquiry* 10 no. 2 [December 1983]: 321–347).

> —Jeanne Heuving. *Omissions Are Not Accidents: Gender in the Art of Marianne Moore* (Detroit: Wayne State University Press, 1992): 124–127.

ELISABETH W. JOYCE ON THE POEM AS MANIFESTO

[Elisabeth W. Joyce teaches at Edinboro University of Pennsylvania. She is the author of *Aesthetics and Cultural Critique: Marianne Moore and the Avant-Garde* in addition to many scholarly articles. Here, Joyce explains the poem as manifesto, linking it to other manifestos, particularly those in the visual arts.]

While Moore inserts quotations from other sources in most of her poetry, the most compelling example of her use of such collage is "Marriage." "Marriage" is her longest poem, the closest she comes to the epic form so prevalent among the modernist poets. Moore's epic, however, has a feminist orientation; she relates social and cultural history through an analysis of the institution of marriage instead of through a focus on public politics and national events. The poem also plays a particularly central role in Moore's oeuvre, mainly because its calculated efforts to question marriage as a viable social institution become a marked emblem of the essentially subversive character of her work. As such, this poem is truly Moore's effort at a manifesto.

"Marriage" begins with a general description of the institution in economic language. The poem then looks at the generic figures of the woman and man, at their gendered personalities. Once these figures have been established, a long discussion between a male and female character ensues which is generally backbiting and nasty, particularly on the part of the female speaker. The poem concludes with an overview of marriage, with highly convoluted language which indicates a type of retreat on Moore's part and her overall disappointment with the marital practice.

Little attention has been paid to the social implications of Moore's poetry, although partly the fault lies with the poet herself. Her continued modesty about her work, especially this poem, and her obscure and teasingly unhelpful notes at the end of her *Complete Poems*, underplay the intensity with which she denigrates social behaviors, from marriage to war. In an interview with Grace Schulman, for instance, Moore described "Marriage" as "just an anthology of words that I didn't want to lose, that I liked very much, and I put them together as plausibly as I could. So people daren't derive a whole philosophy of life from *that*" (qtd. in Schulman 159). In her quiet dismissive manner Moore deflects attention away from the way the poem uses collage to criticize the marital institution.

Moore's disapproval of marriage is most obvious in her poetry notebook at the Rosenbach Museum and Library which shows her revisions and the process involved in her collection of materials, including her notes for "Marriage" and "An Octopus" (Rosenbach 1251/7). A careful analysis of the notebook suggests that a paradoxical doubleness characterizes her collage techniques. Her revisions of her own words tend to mute her disapproval of the marital conventions, while at the same time her revisions of quotations drawn from other sources tend to sharpen her critical stance toward marriage. Much of this critical aspect of her attitude toward marriage can be traced to Moore's alliance to the Dada movement, which had its strong followers in New York (Marcel Duchamp and Francis Picabia, among them), and which also involved iconoclasm and reclamation.

In "Marriage," Moore's recourse to materials from varied sources serves to fracture the formal patterns traditionally associated with poetry and creates instead the rupturing effects of collage. If she had retained conventional poetic forms, she would have upheld the type of "social authority" that the Dadaists were attempting to overthrow. In her presentation of marriage, Moore is anti-lyrical and aphoristic. She undermines lyrical rhythms through the use of random syllabics—this poem is actually unlike her others in its lack of syllable patterning—and through juxtapositions of disparate ideas. The complexity of the dissociated thoughts thrown together in a seeming jumble dissolves the linguistic and thematic harmonies which are so basic to traditions of lyrical poetry. Technical disruptions, then, play into social subversion by severing formal connections with the traditions of the past.

In addition to the quotations which appear in "Marriage," the notebook at the Rosenbach museum includes early drafts of the poem itself. (As Patricia Willis has noted, these early versions of "Marriage" are often conjoined with those of "An Octopus," as if Moore first thought of the two poems as one [247]). Early notes on "Marriage" include statements such as the following which were left out of or were changed for the final version: "This institution should one say enterprise which is universally associated with the fear of loss" (Rosenbach 1251/7: 4,15,22,26); "I don't know what Adam and Eve think of it by this time. / I don't think much of it" (5,13,22); "Its [marriage's] mechanical

advertising / parading as involuntary comment" (13); "Marriage
Is it not like a road uphill in the sand for an aged person?" (18);
"my modern friend who says it is useless / to try to demolish a
thing / until one can identify it" (23). As this last quotation
suggests, if one of the functions of the poem is merely to define
marriage, Moore's purpose is equally to undermine it. Excluded
from the final version of the poem, such remarks are openly
critical of marriage. Clearly Moore felt uncomfortable with
expressing hostility directly and thus turned to methods of
collage which would allow her to retain her disapproval of
marriage, while tempering the intensity of her feelings toward it.

A quotation in "Marriage" continues to bear the meaning it has
in its original source, yet it also carries the new meaning it acquires
it by its position in the poem, by what surrounds it, by the tenor of
the work in general, and by how the poet has cropped it. Moore
reminds us of her quotations' original context by giving references,
albeit vague, in the back of her *Complete Poems*. The overall intent
of the quotation is then changed from its original one, adjusted in
tone, as it were, by the nature of the rest of the poem. Moore
thereby makes a new work of art and makes the tradition of
marriage new, as well, so that both marriage and poetic
conventions can be reassessed for their current value.

—Elisabeth W. Joyce. "The Collage of 'Marriage': Marianne
Moore's Formal and Cultural Critique." *Mosaic* 26, no. 4 (Fall
1993): 108–110.

CRISTANNE MILLER ON MOORE'S CRITIQUE OF HUMAN SELFISHNESS AND COMPROMISE

[Cristanne Miller is the Chair of the English Department
and Coordinator of the American Studies Program at
Pomona College. She is the author of *Emily Dickinson: A
Poet's Grammar*, and *Marianne Moore: Questions of Authority*,
and co-editor of several books of criticism. In this essay,
Miller looks at Moore's poem as a critique of human
selfishness and the subsequent refusal to compromise that
will ruin the institution of marriage.]

The climax of Moore's exploration of the relationships between poetry, gender, and power comes in her 1923 poem "Marriage"—a tour de force of the various poetic strategies that Moore has been perfecting for the last ten or more years.[44] "Marriage" presents an extended portrait of relationships between the sexes, both of a mythical (albeit anachronistically modern) Adam and Eve, and of an anonymous "He" and "She." Far from idealizing either sex, here Moore criticizes both harshly for their failure to see beyond their own selfishness and to remember that the object of their initial desire was a "fight *to be affectionate*" rather than merely "a fight" (my emphasis, Obs, 77).[45] Nonetheless, Moore is more sympathetic to her female character than to her male, and analyzes relationships between them in ways that are notably feminist. Giving Eve precedence of place in the Eden of their mutual independence (she comes first in the poem), Moore also gives Eve linguistic ability equal to, although different from, Adam's: she is "able to write simultaneously / in three languages ... and talk in the meantime" while he is positively "Alive with words" and "prophesie[s] correctly— / the industrious waterfall." Moore, however, also more critically notes that Adam "goes on speaking / in a formal, customary strain" of "everything convenient / to promote one's joy," suggesting the overbearing quality of his fluency. Once the poem has moved fully into the modern world, Moore further admits that Eve's "fight" against selfishness and other forms of human weakness is harder than Adam's, as she must also fight him off—that "spiked hand / that has an affection for one / and proves it to the bone, / impatient to assure you / that impatience is the mark of independence / not of bondage."[46] Although women assert "imperious humility" in the sanctioned space of the tea room, "experience attests / that men have power / and sometimes one is made to feel it" (CP, 77–78).

"Marriage" ends with a long sentence that seems to reflect in its disjunctions and complexity the multiple positionings and almost tortuous desire for fairness of the whole poem. This sentence concludes by describing a statue of Daniel Webster—representative of patriarchy as statesman and orator. A supporter of the Fugitive Slave Act, Webster attempted to preserve the political "Union" which seems here to emblematize the more private union of marriage. Moore begins this sentence by noting the rarity of "that striking grasp of opposites" she so admires in contrast to any static or isolated perspective. Feeling, she then notes, should be similarly complex and variable—a view she characteristically implies by quoting someone who says the opposite:[47]

> "I am such a cow,
> if I had a sorrow,
> I should feel it a long time;
> I am not one of those
> who have a great sorrow
> in the morning
> and a great joy at noon;"
>   (Obs, 80)

The entire poem builds to this indirect insistence on the complexity of living affectionately, sharing a life (and I am inclined to think that much of Moore's experience of this "fight" comes from years of living with her mother), remembering that even the strongest emotions may be followed quickly by their opposite. The poem voices extraordinary suspicion and cynicism about marriage as a public and private enterprise, and perhaps for that reason ends with Daniel Webster as the only possible model for peaceful survival in its state: one must be willing to compromise even deeply held values to remain in this union. The fact that Webster's historic compromise encouraged the continuation of slavery, however, suggests that such union may not finally be desirable. The radical juxtapositions and bricolage of this poem further suggest that Moore, as poet, will not take the kind of settled stand represented by Webster's statue at the end: her shifting and multiple poetic positionings could not be more different from that icon's concrete representation of law, compromise, and public authority.

NOTES

44. For extended readings of this poem, see Keller and Miller's "'The Tooth of Disputation': Marianne Moore's 'Marriage'" (in *Sagetrieb* 6.3 [Winter 1987]: 99–116); Diehl in *American Sublime*; Keller's "'For inferior who is free?'

Liberating the Woman Writer in Marianne Moore's 'Marriage'" (in *Influence and Intertextuality in Literary History*, ed. Jay Clayton and Eric Rothstein [University of Wisconsin Press, 1991], 219–244); Erickson's *Illusion*; Heuving's *Omissions Are Not Accidents*; and Sielke's *Intertextual Networking*.

45. In her working notebook for this poem, Moore notes: "this division into masculine and feminine compartments of achievement will not do" (RML 1251/7).

46. Eileen Moran quotes an early Moore limerick on a similar theme, in reference to Elizabeth Barrett: "There was a young lady named Liz / Who made writing poems her biz / But when she met Bob / She gave up the job / It took all her time to read his" ("Portrait of the Artist: Marianne Moore's Letter to Hildegarde Watson," in *Poesis: A Celebration of H.D. and Marianne Moore* [Bryn Mawr College, 1985], 127; RML 1250/1).

47. Moore reports in correspondence that she does not share the sentiment of this passage: "I did not say 'I am such a cow ...' That was a neighbor" (November 1, 1963, to Mary Schneeberger; from the Macpherson Collection, Ella Strong Denison Library, The Claremont Colleges).

—Cristanne Miller. *Marianne Moore: Questions of Authority* (Cambridge: Harvard University Press, 1995): 118–119.

HEATHER CASS WHITE ON MOORE'S DEFINITION OF CONVERSATION

[Heather Cass White is an Assistant Professor of English at the University of Alabama. She is the author of several scholarly articles. Here, White explains that way in which Moore's particular definition expectations of conversation effects the way in which the poem should be read.]

Commentary on conversation and its role as a guide to her writing runs throughout Moore's prose; often when she writes about literary style and rhythm conversation comes up as the test of each. Moore uses *conversation* to express a range of purposes, including confrontation, subterfuge, artistic expression, politeness, and the exchange of sympathies and ideas. She uses it, to borrow Pamela White Hadas's elegant phrase, to engage in "the fight to be affectionate and the fight not to be" (152). Conversation is a kind of shorthand for Moore's ideas about honesty, naturalness, taste, and the ways in which such moral bearings show through in the work one does. In order to understand how such bearings may become a style, I will first read the moments in her critical prose when she defines the moral and tonal valences that the word *conversation* takes on when she uses it with regard to poetry. These valences include its disparaging resonance when used by her male peers to describe how women spend their time and Moore's reappropriation of the word as a positive description of a complex aesthetic act. On this basis I will then read "Marriage" to elucidate her understanding of a conversational style as a response to her demands of herself to be rigorously and unapologetically true to her gift for invention as well as responsible for the clarity and moral force of her work. (...)

If the poem "Marriage" has a motto, it might well be the 19th line: "we are still in doubt." As an exposition and as an experiment in style, the poem asks the same question: is the "striking grasp of opposites / opposed each to the other, not to unity," an "amalgamation which can never be more / than an interesting impossibility" (73)? Expositionally, it wonders about the possibility of amalgamating in marriage public and private, institution and enterprise, man and woman, individual and community. Stylistically it combines "experiment," "fine art," "ritual," and "recreation" (76) in conjoining its disparate tools: allusion, metaphor, citation, and epigrammatic commentary. This combination is itself an uneasy marriage, which verges frequently on unintelligibility as competing modes work side by side. Like the idea of marriage that the poem investigates, the poem itself keeps asking whether the "disputation" (77) by which it must prove itself is a fight that will tear it apart or a conversation that will bind it together, in however uneasy a peace.

In this sense, the question of how "plausibly" the poet manages to arrange her different poetic materials is of the essence. Like a good conversationalist, she should be able to inflect each change in tone, image, idea, and method so that the whole to which they contribute has a discernible shape that does not distort any one of its elements. The possibility of achieving such a balance is an issue that concerns Moore from some of her earliest poems onward.[11] "Marriage" poses the problem of complexity that must not become murkiness, either formally or thematically. Formally, as we have seen, it moves in undemarcated, rapid-fire transitions between stylistic methods, principally allusion, metaphor, citation, and epigram, challenging the reader and the poet to find the "hidden principle" by which they may be understood to belong to the same poem. Thematically, it concerns the confusion that results when Adam and Eve talk to each other, implicitly asking if their conversations can be understood to constitute the "unity" of marriage. More specifically, it asks what efficacy "politeness" can have in making conversationalists out of these opposed people, who stand in unequal relations to the social structures of the world they inhabit.

NOTE

11. For example, one can trace in such poems as "Diligence Is to Magic as Progress Is to Flight," "To a Snail," and "In the Days of Prismatic Color" the history of Moore's concern that her delight in invention, compression, and complexity will make her poetry needlessly obscure.

—Heather Cass White. "Morals, Manners, and 'Marriage': Marianne Moore's Art of Conversation." *Twentieth Century Literature* 45, no. 4 (Winter 1999): 490, 499–500.

Marianne Moore

Poems, 1921.

Marriage, 1923.

Observations, 1924, revised 1925.

Selected Poems, 1935.

The Pangolin and Other Verse, 1936.

What Are Years?, 1941.

Nevertheless, 1944.

A Face, 1949.

Collected Poems, 1951.

The Fables of La Fontaine, translated by Moore, 1954.

Predilections, 1955.

Like a Bulwark, 1956.

Idiosyncrasy & Technique, 1958.

Letters To and From the Ford Motor Company, by Moore and David Wallace, 1958.

O To Be A Dragon, 1959.

A Marianne Moore Reader, 1961.

The Absentee (Moore's dramatic interpretation of Maria Edgeworth's novel), 1962.

Eight Poems, 1963.

Occasionem Cognosce, 1963.

Puss in Boots, The Sleeping Beauty & Cinderella: A Reteling of Three Classic Fairy Tales, Based on the French of Charles Perrault, 1963.

Rock Crystal, A Christmas Tale, by Adalbert Stifter, translated by Moor and Elizabeth Mayer, 1964, revised 1965.

The Arctic Fox, 1964.

Poetry and Criticism, 1965.

Dress and Kindred Subjects, 1965.

A Talisman, 1965.

Silence, 1965.

Tell Me, Tell Me: Granite, Steel, and Other Topics, 1966.

Tippo's Tiger, 1967.

The Complete Poems of Marianne Moore, 1968.

Selected Poems, 1969.

The Accented Syllable, 1969.

Prevalent at One Time, 1970.

The Complete Poems of Marianne Moore, ed. Clive E. Driver and Patricia C. Willis, posthumously published 1981.

Answers to Some Questions Posed By Howard Nemerov, 1982.

Marianne Moore

Abbott, Craig S. *Marianne Moore, A Reference Guide*. Boston: G.K. Hall, 1978.

Bloom, Harold, ed. *Modern Critical Views: Marianne Moore*. New York: Chelsea House Publishers, 1987.

Costello, Bonnie. *Marianne Moore: Imaginary Possessions*. Cambridge, MA: Harvard University Press, 1981.

Davis, Alex and Lee M. Jenkins, eds. *Locations of Literary Modernism: Region and Nation in British and American Modernist Poetry*. Cambridge: Cambridge University Press, 2000.

Diehl, Joanne Feit. *Elizabeth Bishop and Marianne Moore: The Psychodynamics of Creativity*. Princeton: Princeton University Press, 1993.

Doreski, William. "Williams and Moore: History and the Colloquial Style." *The Modern Voice in American Poetry*. Gainesville: University Press of Florida, 1995.

Engel, Bernard F. *Marianne Moore, Revised Edition*. Boston: Twayne Publishers, 1989.

Erickson, Darlene Williams. *Illusion Is More Precise Than Precision: The Poetry of Marianne Moore*. Tuscaloosa: The University of Alabama Press, 1992.

Garrigue, Jean. *Marianne Moore*. Minneapolis: University of Minnesota Press, 1965.

Goodridge, Celeste. *Hints and Disguises: Marianne Moore and Her Contemporaries*. Iowa City: University of Iowa Press, 1989.

Gregory, Elizabeth. *Quotation and Modern American Poetry: Imnaginary Gardens with Read Toads*. Houston: Rice University Press, 1996.

Hadas, Pamela White. *Marianne Moore: Poet of Affection*. Syracuse: Syracuse University Press, 1977.

Hall, Donald. *Marianne Moore: The Cage and The Animal*. New York: Pegasus, 1970.

Heuving, Jeanne. *Omissions Are Not Accidents: Gender in the Art of Marianne Moore*. Detroit: Wayne State University Press, 1992.

Holley, Margaret. *The Poetry of Marianne Moore: A Study in Voice and Value*. Cambridge: Cambridge University Press, 1987.

Joyce, Elisabeth. "The Collage of 'Marriage': Marianne Moore's Formal and Cultural Critique." *Mosiac* 26, no. 4 (Fall 1993): 103–118.

Lakritz, Andrew M. *Modernism and the Other in Stevens, Frost and Moore*. Gainesville: University of Florida Press, 1996.

Leavell, Linda. *Marianne Moore and the Visual Arts: Prismatic Color*. Baton Rouge: Louisiana State University Press, 1995.

Marianne Moore Newsletter. Editor Patricia C. Willis. Philadelphia: Rosenbach Foundation, 1977–1983.

Martin, Taffy. *Marianne Moore: Subversive Modernist*. Austin: University of Texas Press, 1986.

Merrin, Jeredith. *An Enabling Humility: Marianne Moore, Elizabeth Bishop and the Uses of Tradition*. New Brunswick, NJ: Rutgers University Press, 1990.

Miller, Cristanne. *Marianne Moore: Questions of Authority*. Cambridge: Harvard University Press, 1995.

Molesworth, Charles. *Marianne Moore: A Literary Life*. New York: Antheneum, 1990.

Nitchie, George W. *Marianne Moore: An Introduction to the Poetry*. New York: Columbia University Press, 1969.

Parisi, Joseph, ed. *Marianne Moore: The Art of a Modernist*. Ann Arbor, The University of Michigan Research Press, 1990.

Paul, Catherine E. *Poetry in the Museums of Modernism*. Ann Arbor: The University of Michigan Press, 2002.

Phillips, Elizabeth. *Marianne Moore*. New York: Frederick Ungar Publishing Co., 1982.

Poesis: A Journal of Criticism 6, nos. 3 and 4 (1985). Special Moore/H.D. issue.

Quarterly Review of Literature 4, no. 2 (1948). Special Moore issue.

Qian, Zhaoming. *The Modernist Response to Chinese Art: Pound, Moore, Stevens*. Charlottesville: University of Virginia Press, 2003.

Rotella, Guy L. *Reading and Writing Nature: The Poetry of Robert Frost, Wallace Stevens, Marianne Moore, and Elizabeth Bishop*. Boston: Northeastern University Press, 1991.

Schulman, Grace. *Marianne Moore: The Poetry of Engagement.* Urbana and Chicago: University of Illinois Press, 1986.

———. "Conversation with Marianne Moore." *Quarterly Review of Literature* 16 (1969): 154–171.

Schulze, Robin. *Becoming Marianne Moore: The Early Poems, 1907–1924.* Berkeley, University of California Press, 2002.

———. *The Web of Friendship: Marianne Moore and Wallace Stevens.* Ann Arbor: University of Michigan Press, 1995.

Sielke, Sabine. *Fashioning the Female Subject: The Intertextual Networking of Dickinson, Moore and Rich.* Ann Arbor: University of Michigan Press, 1997.

Slatin, John M. *The Savage's Romance: The Poetry of Marianne Moore.* State College, PA: The Pennsylvania State University Press, 1986.

Stamy, Cynthia. *Marianne Moore and China: Orientalism and a Writing of America.* Oxford: Oxford University Press, 1999.

Stapleton, Laurence. *Marianne Moore: The Poet's Advance.* Princeton: Princeton University Press, 1978.

Tomlinson, Charles, ed. *Marianne Moore: A Collection of Critical Essays.* Englewood Cliffs, NJ: Prentice Hall, 1969.

Weatherhead, A. Kingsley. *The Edge of the Image: Marianne Moore, William Carlos Williams and Some Other Poets.* Seattle: University of Washington Press, 1967.

Willis, Patricia C., ed. *Marianne Moore: Woman and Poet.* Orono, Maine: The National Poetry Foundation, University of Maine, 1990.

Zona, Kirstin Hotelling. *Marianne Moore, Elizabeth Bishop and May Swenson: The Feminist Poetics of Self-Restraint.* Ann Arbor: The University of Michigan Press, 2002.

ACKNOWLEDGMENTS

"Marianne Moore" by A. Kingsley Weatherhead. From *The Edge of the Image: Marianne Moore, Williams Carlos Williams, and Some Other Poets* by A. Kingsley Weatherhead. © 1967 by the University of Washington Press. Reprinted by permission.

"Ut Pictura Poesis: Moore and the Visual Arts" by Bonnie Costello. From *Marianne Moore: Imaginary Possessions* by Bonnie Costello. © 1981 by the President and Fellows of Harvard College. Reprinted by permission.

"A Reason for Living in a Town Like This" by John M. Slatin. From *The Savage's Romance* by John M. Slatin. © 1986 by the Pennsylvania State University Press. Reprinted by permission.

"The Armored Self: Selected Poems" by Bernard F. Engel. From *Marianne Moore: Revised Edition* by Bernard F. Engel. © 1988 by G. K. Hall & Co. All rights reserved. Reprinted by permission of the Gale Group.

"Idiom and Idiosyncracy" by Robert Pinsky. From *Marianne Moore: The Art of a Modernist*. Ed. Jay Parisi. © 1990 by The University of Michigan Press. Reprinted by permission.

"Marianne Moore" by Guy Rotella. From *Reading and Writing Nature* by Guy Rotella. © 1991 by Northeastern University Press. Reprinted by permission.

"A Poet That Matters" by Robin G. Schulze. From *Web of Friendship* by Robin G. Schulze. © 1995 by the University of Michigan Press. Reprinted by permission.

"The Experience of the Eye" by Hugh Kenner. From *The Southern Review* 1 (October 1965). © 1965 by *The Southern Review*. Reprinted by permission.

"Crafstmanship Disfigured and Restored" by Taffy Martin. From *Marianne Moore: Subversive Modernist* by Taffy Martin. © 1986 by the University of Texas Press. Reprinted by permission.

INDEX OF
Themes and Ideas